COUNTIES OF
NORTHERN
MARYLAND

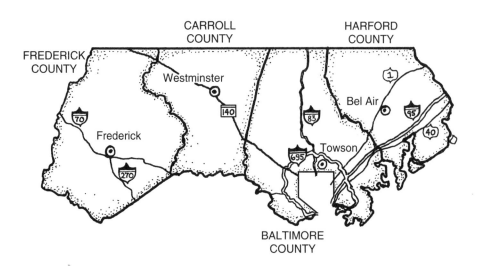

OUR MARYLAND COUNTIES SERIES

COUNTIES OF NORTHERN MARYLAND

by Elaine Bunting & Patricia D'Amario

Elaine Bunting   *Patricia D'Amario*

Tidewater Publishers
Centreville, Maryland

Library of Congress Cataloging-in-Publication Data

Bunting, Elaine
    Counties of northern Maryland / by Elaine Bunting & Patricia D'Amario.—1st ed.
      p. cm. — (Our Maryland counties series.)
    Includes bibliographical references (p.) and index.
    Summary: Presents information about the history, geography, climate, famous people, natural resources, and points of interest of Maryland's four northern counties.
    ISBN 0-87033-520-0
    1. Maryland—Juvenile literature. 2. Baltimore County (Md.)—Juvenile literature. 3. Frederick County (Md.)—Juvenile literature. 4. Harford County (Md.)—Juvenile literature. 5. Carroll County (Md.)—Juvenile literature. [1. Maryland. 2. Baltimore County (Md.) 3. Frederick County (Md.) 4. Harford County (Md.) 5. Carroll County (Md.)] I. D'Amario, Patricia. II. Title. III. Series: Bunting, Elaine Our Maryland counties series.

F181.3.B864 2000
975.2′7—dc21

99-058076

Manufactured in the United States of America
First edition

To Helen and Eugene Buchler, my parents, whose love, humor, and boundless high spirits served as my inspiration and guidance through the years

—P.D.

To my aunt and uncle, Nadine and Milton Hudson, for their encouragement and support

—E.B.

CONTENTS

COUNTY SEALS

Baltimore County

Baltimore County's seal looks very much like the Maryland flag. It is round with the Crossland and Calvert coats of arms in the middle. There are seven stars in the center representing the seven election districts. Designed by Adelaide M. Haspert, it became the official seal of the county on June 10, 1957.

Frederick County

The original seal of Frederick County dates back to the late 1800s. It was redesigned in May 1957. This new seal represents the historic character as well as the agricultural and industrial development of the county. It shows a farmer with a stalk of grain in his left hand and a scythe in his right hand. A factory is also shown against a background of mountains. Thirteen stars form an arch over the picture, which is in red and black. Below the picture is the date, 1748.

Harford County

The coat of arms of Harford County was designed by George Van Bibber. The gold color stands for "the wealth of the county and the richness of its fields." Three bands of blue represent the three major streams that run through the county—Deer Creek, Winters Run, and Bynum Run. A white quill pen honors those who wrote and signed the Bush Declaration. A sword represents defense materials produced at Aberdeen Proving Ground and Edgewood Arsenal. Below the shield are the words "At the risque of our lives and fortunes," the last line of the Bush Declaration. The coat of arms was adopted in 1964 by a vote of the county commissioners.

Carroll County

The county seal of Carroll County dates from June 5, 1837, when the county tax commissioners designated money for a seal. However, the seal did not become official until July 1, 1977, 140 years later. At the center of the seal is a freight wagon drawn by four horses. The year 1837 is written above the wagon. The colors in the seal are red, white, brown, and blue.

PREFACE

In earlier years, Maryland had fewer counties than it has today. Counties such as Baltimore and Frederick covered extremely large areas of land. In northern Maryland, settlements grew along the Chesapeake Bay, Susquehanna River, and smaller lakes and streams. These provided an easy way to transport goods to faraway settlements and towns.

The county seat was the center for government and business. As populations increased, people did not want to travel great distances over poor roads to conduct their transactions. Public demand grew to carve out additional counties, first from Baltimore, then from Frederick. This is the story of the northern Maryland region, tracing the formation of Baltimore, Frederick, Harford, and Carroll counties, and describing them as they are today.

Our thanks to the staff of the Maryland Hall of Records in Annapolis.

In Baltimore County: Thank you to the staff of the Baltimore County Public Library in Towson, particularly Susan Bath; Elmer R. Haile, Jr., and John McGrain, Historical Society of Baltimore County; William E. Allen, Chief Deputy Clerk of Circuit Court for Baltimore County; Brittany White, Baltimore County Conference and Business Bureau; and William Dee, tour guide at Hampton National Historic Site.

In Frederick County: Thank you to the staff of the Frederick County Public Library in Frederick, particularly Julia Cubit, Reference Librarian; Janet Houch and Gloria Routzahn, Tourism Council of Frederick County; Gayle Marie Denny, Paul E. Fogle, Marie Washburn, and Nancy Leasure of the Historical Society of Frederick County; Virginia

Danko, County Clerk for the District Court of Frederick County; Charlie Keller, Clerk of Circuit Court of Frederick County; Mary Alice Shankle, court clerk's office; Rebecca A. Crebbs, county manager's office; Belinda K. Teague, Executive Assistant to the Frederick County Commissioners; the staff of the Frederick County Chamber of Commerce; and Stephen O'Phillips, Department of Planning and Zoning. Thank you to Herbert Whiteley, who worked on the Carroll Creek Flood Control Project.

In Harford County: Thank you to Marlene Magness, Jim Chrismer, James Dorsey, Mabel Andrews, and Thirza M. Brandt, Historical Society of Harford County; Charlotte Cronin, Anna Duguid, and Ruth Duguid, The Aberdeen Room Archives and Museum; Carol Sweet, Administrative Clerk of the District Court of Harford County; Jane (last name withheld by request), Administrative Clerk of the Circuit Court of Harford County; Eileen Lewis, Office of Economic Development in Bel Air; Frank Lopez, Maryland Forest Service in Bel Air; Corporal Cochran, Maryland State Police, Benson Barrack; Ralph Gullion, Harford County Sheriff's Department; Karen Gyolai, American Association of University Women, Harford Branch; and Frank Hawley, George Twombly, and Jim McMahan, Ripken Museum in Aberdeen.

In Carroll County: Thank you to the staff of the Carroll County Public Library in Westminster; Jay Graybeal, Director, Historical Society of Carroll County, and Susan Bundy, library volunteer; the staff of the Carroll County Chamber of Commerce; and the bailiff at the historic courthouse (name withheld by request).

COUNTIES OF NORTHERN MARYLAND

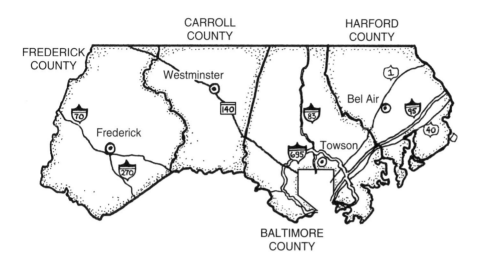

OVERVIEW OF NORTHERN MARYLAND

The counties of Baltimore, Frederick, Harford, and Carroll lie along Maryland's northern border with Pennsylvania.

At one time, much of northern Maryland was called Baltimore County. Though it had no specific boundaries, the county covered a large area in northeastern and central Maryland, including part of the Eastern Shore. Another early county, Prince George's, spanned sections of central and western Maryland. In 1674, the size of Baltimore County was reduced when Cecil became the first county to separate. Frederick was formed from a part of Prince George's County in 1748. Harford County

Maryland is the only state in the United States with a Baltimore County or a Harford County. However, Virginia has a Frederick County, and there are Carroll Counties in Arkansas, Georgia, Illinois, Indiana, Iowa, Kentucky, Maryland, Mississippi, Missouri, New Hampshire, Ohio, Tennessee, and Virginia.

FUN FACT

then separated from Baltimore County in 1773, and Carroll County was formed from Baltimore and Frederick counties in 1837.

Geography and Climate

Baltimore County covers 612 square miles, making it the third largest county in Maryland. It has 173 miles of shoreline with 638 square miles of land and water.

The fall line (the geographical place where the land changes from the Atlantic Coastal Plain to the Piedmont Plateau) is evident at such places as the falls on the Gunpowder River. Elevations in the county range from sea level to 1,000 feet, though most of the county lies between 200 and 700 feet.

The average winter temperature in Baltimore County is 34.9 degrees and the average summer temperature is 74.1 degrees. Average annual precipitation is 46.7 inches.

Frederick County is Maryland's largest county, covering 664.1 square miles. It extends from the Pennsylvania state line on the north to the Potomac River at the south. The geography of Frederick County can be divided into two separate types of terrain (land forms) that meet in the center of the county. To the east of the Blue Ridge Mountains is the Piedmont Plateau, which is higher than the coastal plain. This plateau has rolling hills, fast-moving streams, and narrow valleys. West of the Blue Ridge is the Appalachian region.

There are six square miles of water in the county. The Monocacy, the Potomac, and the Catoctin Rivers run through the county. There are also many creeks and "runs" such as Little Owens Creek, Sandy Run, Little Fishing Creek, Muddy Run, Glade Creek, Tuscarora Creek, and Cattail Creek.

Elevations range from 294 feet to 1,895 feet above sea level. Two mountain ranges, which parallel the Monocacy River, run through Frederick County. The Catoctin Mountains and South Mountain are both part of the Blue Ridge section of the larger Appalachian mountain range. They form two valleys in the county. Middletown Valley lies between South Mountain and the Catoctin Mountains. The Monocacy Valley lies east of the Catoctin Mountains. Blue Ridge or South Mountain extends along the western boundary of the county, dividing Frederick and Washington counties. Several times in its geological history, this area has been under an inland sea. The mountain ranges were pushed up by forces beneath the earth. The mountains were at one time much higher, but have eroded over time.

Temperatures in the county range from the average 36.6 degrees in the winter to an average 73.4 degrees in the summer. The annual precipitation averages 40.8 inches, and yearly snowfall averages 26.4 inches.

Harford County's geography rises from the fairly flat coastal plain to the hilly Piedmont region located in the distinct area known as the fall line. This line is marked by the change in elevation of the land and also by the rocks and waterfalls that begin to appear along rivers and streams. In Harford County, the fall line roughly follows Interstate 95. The elevation of the county varies from about 20 feet above sea level near Havre de Grace to about 700 near Norrisville.

The main rivers are the Susquehanna, the Gunpowder, and the Bush. The abundance of streams, creeks, and runs in the county led to the rise of the mill industry in the 1700s and 1800s. At one time there were about one hundred of these mills in the county. Today, only about a dozen are still standing.

Many small streams have funny names. Some of them are Graveyard Creek, Ha Ha Branch, Cabbage Run, and Bread and Cheese Branch. *FUN FACT*

There are approximately 453 square miles of land in the county. The northern half of the county is largely agricultural. It has rich soil, good for the growing of crops. The growing season lasts an average of 187 days.

The southern part of Harford County is suburban. Many people live there and commute to jobs in Baltimore via Interstate 95 or Route 40. New homes have been built to accommodate the growing number of people moving to Harford County.

Northern Maryland has a mild, humid climate, though extreme temperatures have occurred. An average 45 inches of rain falls each year in Harford County.

Carroll County has a land area of 456 square miles. It measures about 27 miles in both width and length.

Carroll County is hilly and has many streams flowing through its valleys. Two ridges known as Parr's Ridge and Dug Hill form a divide in the county. Streams to the east of this ridge flow in a southeasterly direction to the Patapsco and Gunpowder rivers. Streams to the west of the ridge flow southwest to the Monocacy River and then to the Potomac River. This diagonal division between Parr's Ridge and Dug Hill separates the Piedmont region into its eastern and western sections.

Elevations range from 300 feet above sea level in the southeast to 1,080 feet near Dug Hill in the northeast section of the county.

The county's temperate climate is influenced by the nearby Chesapeake Bay and the Atlantic Ocean. A growing season of 165 to 200 days explains why Carroll County is so well known for its agriculture. The fertile soil contributes to the county's agricultural success.

Wildlife

There are many different kinds of wildlife in **Baltimore, Frederick, Harford,** and **Carroll** counties.

Common varieties of birds found in this northern Maryland region include northern cardinals, mockingbirds, robins, sparrows, owls, crows, blue jays, barn swallows, catbirds, black-capped chickadees, goldfinches, purple finches, eastern bluebirds, ruby-throated hummingbirds, and juncos. There are also shore birds such as mallard ducks, egrets, belted kingfishers, Canada geese, ospreys, wood ducks, and herons. Rarer birds include wild turkeys, pheasants, flickers and other woodpeckers, American bald eagles, and Baltimore orioles.

Common mammals in the area are raccoons, beavers, cottontail rabbits, deer, red foxes, gray foxes, opossums, squirrels, chipmunks, groundhogs, and coyotes. (Yes, coyotes have been spotted in Harford County.) Black bears are returning to the area.

Reptiles and amphibians in the area include turtles, salamanders, snakes (including water snakes and poisonous copperheads), frogs, and toads.

Fish include large- and smallmouth bass, striped bass (rockfish), crappie, channel catfish, yellow and white perch, bluegill sunfish, carp, shad, and chain pickerel and trout.

In Harford and Baltimore counties, crabs, clams, and oysters are harvested and sold throughout Maryland and other states around the country.

Frederick County has some endangered animals, including the common moorhen, the least bittern, the green floater, the shrike, the sora, and the Pizzini's Cave amphipod.

Plants

Baltimore, Frederick, Harford, and **Carroll** counties have a variety of trees found in moist deciduous forests. Some of these include various maples, beech, elm, hemlock, hickory, oak, black walnut, tulip poplar, alder, black cherry, sycamore, white spruce, northern white cedar, ash, black birch, flowering dogwood, and black locust. Evergreens include Japanese holly, American holly, pine (various kinds), fir, and northern white cedar.

Large tree farms of white and red pine are found in Frederick and Baltimore counties. A tree farm is a forest where almost all the trees were planted by man.

Herbaceous plants such as marsh marigold, skunk cabbage, yellow lady's slipper, violet, Greek valerian, and Canada lily grow in the area.

Some shrubs, bushes, and vines in the area are mountain laurel, multifloral rose, Japanese honeysuckle, white mulberry, osage orange, rosebay rhododendron, sweet fern shrub, winterberry shrub, yew, spicebush, alder, and the turtlehead.

Jack-in-the-pulpit, black-eyed Susan, moss, ferns, and cattails are a few of the other plants that are found in the northern Maryland region.

Underwater plants are found in the northern Chesapeake Bay and rivers such as the Susquehanna, Bush, and Gunpowder. These are known as submerged aquatic vegetation (SAV), and they include eelgrass, redhead grass, sago pondweed, wild celery, and widgeon grass. These grasses are vitally important since they provide the habitat and food supply for fish and waterfowl.

Frederick County has some endangered plants such as coastal Juneberry, mosquito fern, Indian paintbrush, red turtlehead, and Bradley's spleenwort.

EARLY NORTHERN MARYLAND

The first evidence of prehistoric animals in Maryland was found in Frederick County at Emmitsburg. Recently, footprints were found in a sandstone rock there. Each footprint is four inches wide, has three toes, and is webbed like the foot of a duck. According to paleontologists (people who study fossils and geological periods), these footprints were formed during the Triassic period (212–228 million years ago). Red Triassic sandstones have also been found in Carroll and Montgomery counties.

In February 1998, nuns at the Provincial House of the Daughters of Charity in Emmitsburg showed a thousand-pound rock that had been stored in their barn for over one hundred years. This rock has over two dozen three-toed dinosaur footprints on its surface.   *FUN FACT*

Native Peoples

The Paleolithic culture (prehistoric) was the earliest known to have lived in northern Maryland. These nomadic hunter-gatherers lived there ten to twelve thousand years ago and roamed the length of the East Coast. Archaeologists (those who study the remains of early cultures) have also found traces of Native American (Indian) life from about five thousand years ago in the northern Maryland area.

In the early Archaic period (8000 B.C. to 1000 B.C.), the climate was warmer than in the Paleolithic era. The natives lived mostly along creeks and streams, hunting deer and small mammals. In the Monocacy Valley, however, there is evidence that they moved away from rivers. By the late Woodland period (A.D. 900 to A.D. 1600), natives were living in large villages along major rivers and growing maize (corn).

The Susquehannocks were known for their great size. George Alsop, who lived among them, described them as "large and warlike—for the most part seven foot tall—voices deep and hollow as coming out of a cave." They were part of the Iroquois nation. They built temporary settlements in what is now Harford County and a larger, more permanent settlement in what is now Cecil County. They also lived along the Susquehanna River in Pennsylvania and traveled south to hunt and fish. The Susquehannocks considered their hunting grounds to include the area from north of the Maryland-Pennsylvania line to the Patuxent River. They often fought with neighboring tribes of Piscataways, Senecas, and Nanticokes for hunting rights in northern Maryland. Native cabins used only for hunting were discovered in this area in the late 1600s.

Because they were hunters, these native people ate venison (deer meat), rabbit, and fish. They were also farmers who grew beans, tobacco, maize, and melons. They prepared the maize in a variety of ways. It could be used as a vegetable, and it could also be made into bread. In addition, they ate bird's eggs, wild plants, berries, nuts, and fruit.

One of the main reasons the earliest settlers came to the northern parts of the Chesapeake Bay was to trade with the Native Americans, but the Susquehannocks (sometimes spelled Susquehannoughs) occasionally attacked the settlers.

Although the Susquehannocks were mighty warriors, their final battle was against an enemy they could not defeat. After twelve years of war with the Senecas and the Cayugas, they were attacked by smallpox, a terrible disease that causes blisters on the skin and in many cases, results in death. By 1673, only three hundred warriors were left in the upper Chesapeake area of Baltimore, Harford, and Cecil counties. These were driven south toward Virginia by their enemies, but they returned north to Pennsylvania again. The last few were put to death in Lancaster Jail in 1763 after massacres committed by some of them turned the white colonists against all the natives in the area. Eventually, the smaller tribes were defeated, and they moved away from northern Maryland. By 1773, colonists could settle with little fear of the natives.

Around 1697, the Conoy tribe, part of the Algonquian nation, lived and explored the hills, streams, and springs of Frederick County. There is evidence of the Conoys near Point of Rocks on the Potomac River. Harassed by other tribes, they left their villages and made temporary homes along the Potomac River. By 1712, the Conoys and Tuscaroras moved to more permanent locations in Pennsylvania and New York. Artifacts from Iroquois tribes have also been found in the area.

At this time, there were so many fish in northern Maryland that the waters swarmed with them. Natives could catch as many as thirty sturgeon (a variety of large fish) in one night. The woods were also teeming with buffalo, deer, bears, and turkeys.   *FUN FACT*

In the early days of Carroll and Frederick counties, the land was covered mostly by forests. Not much is really known about the natives of this area, but there are two theories. One is that the natives did not live in the area but only camped there to go hunting. Because of the great number of artifacts found in the area, the other theory is that a large number of natives did live there permanently. There have been recent findings of village sites in the Monocacy Valley. It is known that Susquehannocks farmed there. They were generally friendly with the early settlers with whom they traded furs.

It is believed that the last Native Americans to live in Frederick County were Susquehannocks, and they were gone by 1751.

The Tuscarora tribe used Carroll County as their hunting grounds, particularly the area that is now Taneytown. They hunted deer, beavers, wolves, otters, bears, and wildcats. Other tribes such as the Iroquois, Conoy, Piscataway, Delaware, and Shawnee are also known to have hunted in the area.

Many place names are derived from Native American words. "Chesapeake" had several possible meanings, among them "mother of waters" and "a country on a great river." The village of Shawan in Baltimore County was named after a tribe of Indians who camped at this area when they traveled to and from Pennsylvania.

Exploration

There was exploration by the Spanish in 1588. The first recorded exploration was by Captain John Smith. He made two voyages from the Jamestown, Virginia, area in 1608. He wanted to explore the rivers and bays to the north. His first trip lasted less than three weeks. He traveled as far north as the Patapsco River. His second trip brought him to what is now Harford County. During this second voyage, Captain Smith explored the Bush River, the Susquehanna River, and a smaller river off the Susquehanna believed to be Deer Creek. Captain Smith was very impressed with the beautiful land he saw from the rivers he explored in this area.

William Claiborne came to northern Maryland from Virginia also. He later settled on an island located at the place where the Susquehanna River empties into the Chesapeake Bay.

It is thought that the first white men to enter the area that is now Frederick and Carroll counties were Frenchmen who came with some Shawnee tribesmen about 1692. Hunters and trappers had been in the area about 1700, and Swiss explorer Franz Louis Michel was there about 1702, but the area was not seriously explored until around 1709. Sugarloaf Mountain was explored and climbed during the early 1700s.

During their explorations, Captain Smith and his crew named the places they saw   *FUN FACT*
after themselves. Two examples are Smith's Falls on the
Susquehanna and Powell's Isle (now Poole's Island), part
of the Edgewood Arsenal.

...And this is Smith Falls, on the Smith River, by Smith Mountain, near Smith Valley...

Settlement by Europeans

The first known settlement in the northern
Maryland area was founded by Edward
Palmer on a small island at the mouth of
the Susquehanna River about 1622. Palmer
was a young Englishman seeking wealth and
adventure and a place to build a university.
Why he would choose such a remote place to build a university is unknown, and he and his followers did not stay long.

In 1625, King James had given George Calvert the title of Baron of
Baltimore, the first Lord Baltimore. After the death of King James,
King Charles I offered Calvert the land near Virginia that would become "Terra Mariae"—Maryland. Lord Baltimore died before the king
had signed the charter (the official paper transferring ownership of the
land), but Calvert's son Cecil (the second Lord Baltimore) took over
the land and actually signed the charter agreement in 1632. Calvert
owned all of Maryland, including the island settled by Palmer.

Shortly before Calvert took ownership, William Claiborne, another
young Englishman, had set up a fur-trading post on the island.
Claiborne had come from Virginia because the governor had asked him
to explore farther north in the Chesapeake Bay. He heard John Smith's
stories of the area and thought he could get rich there. Claiborne befriended the natives and was much more successful with the fur-trading
business than Edward Palmer had been. However, since the island now
belonged to Lord Baltimore, Claiborne's claim was illegal.

Though William Claiborne had gotten along well with the Indians
in the area, when Calvert took over, he sent men to defend the island
from the natives. They built a fort and armed it with men and weapons.
They also built storage houses for the fishing industry and cleared land
for agriculture.

The name Palmer's Island was eventually changed to Watson's Island, then to Garrett Island, named for the president of the Baltimore and Ohio Railroad. (The B&O built supports for a railroad bridge on the island in 1885.)

It is believed that the earliest settlers came to the **Baltimore County** area in the 1650s. Many of these colonists were English. They settled at the northern end of the Chesapeake Bay in what is now Cecil and Harford counties. These early settlements were the result of huge land grants from Lord Baltimore. They were rewards for loyalty and gifts to friends. Most of these land grants included many hundreds of acres. All were along the coastline of the Bay or its rivers. The settlers traveled long distances between settlements, and it was easier to go by water.

Some of the early grants were Poole's Island to Captain Robert Morris in 1659; Cranberry Hall on the east side of the Bush River to John Hall in 1694; and Bearson's Island, near what is now Havre de Grace, to Nathaniel Utie in 1658.

FUN FACT	Some other grants with interesting names were Mosquito Proof, Beaver Neck, Woodpecker, Gum Neck, Satan, The Stop, Cranberry Hill, and Penny Come Quick.

The Bearson's Island grant was one of the largest, with 2,300 acres. Colonel Nathaniel Utie changed the name to Spesutie to mean "Utie's Hope." It eventually became known as Spesutia.

Between 1650 and 1664, there was some settlement along sections of the shoreline of the Chesapeake Bay and the lower Patapsco River. However, Baltimore County did not grow very fast. Before 1663, there were so few people that the county did not need a pillory (also called stocks). The pillory was a device used to punish criminals. It was a wooden frame with holes into which the prisoner's head, hands, and feet could be locked.

Lord Baltimore granted land and also rented it. People visited each other by boat, and farmers shipped their produce to market by boat. After 1664, settlement spread farther along the Bay and rivers. Charles Calvert, the third Lord Baltimore, had 7,031 acres of land surveyed between the Big and Little Gunpowder rivers. He kept this land for himself. It was called "His Lordship's Manor in the Forks of the

Gunpowder." Gradually, the land away from the water was surveyed and settled, but not until after 1700. The interior was heavily wooded, making it difficult to cut roads.

One settler in the area that is now Baltimore County was Daniel Dulany. He came to America as an indentured servant. These were people whose passage to America had been paid by an "employer." The indentured person was then required to work as a servant for a certain number of years. Dulany worked for Richard Smith, who owned the tract of land called Jehosophat. Dulany married Smith's daughter. The family remained loyal to England during the American Revolution. At the end of the war, their land was taken over by the new Maryland government.

My Lady's Manor (originally called Lord Baltimore's Guift) was a 10,000-acre land grant. Charles Calvert gave it to his fourth wife, Margaret, in 1713. After her death, the land was rented to farmers.

In the early 1700s, Baltimore County was still sparsely settled, with fewer than five hundred families living there.

The oldest building still standing in Baltimore County is Fort Garrison, established in 1693. A captain and six rangers used it to watch for Indian attacks, which probably never came.   *FUN FACT*

By the beginning of the 1700s, settlers became interested in **Frederick County.** One of these settlers was the French trader Cartier. He married a native girl and settled near the mouth of the Monocacy in 1711. Others included John Van Metre, a constable who settled in 1724; Thomas Albin, who was a squatter (living there illegally); Josiah Ballinger, who settled near Buckeystown; and Sir George Swinehart, who settled at Monocacy in 1732.

In the early 1700s, land grants were given to English-speaking people who already lived in Maryland. It is believed that many settlers came to Frederick County from Prince George's, Charles, and St. Mary's counties. Some others came from Virginia, Pennsylvania, Delaware, and New York as well as England, Scotland, and Ireland. They settled in the southern part of the county and in the Monocacy and Middletown valleys. A few German settlers came as early as 1710. The first survey of land (called Hope) within today's Frederick County was made in November 1721. This land belonged to William Fitzredmond, who was the nephew of Charles Carroll and a business associate of Daniel Dulany. The second survey of land (Carrollton) was recorded in April 1723 for Charles Carroll, the settler. He bought this land for his children from the native people in the area.

FUN FACT   Some land grants in Frederick County in the 1700s had unusual names such as Ask and Ye Shall Receive, All Disputes Settled, All Neighbors Confused, Hard Bargain, First Come First Served, Lost Kitty, Shoemaker's Tricks, Who Could Have Thoughtit, Punch Spoon, and We Have Got the Bird in the Cage.

The first black man to receive a land grant from Lord Baltimore in Frederick County was John Dorsey in 1743. The land was located in what is now New Market.

Sometimes, people who owned large parcels of land did not actually live there. They were known as absentee landowners. Before 1732, most of these parcels averaged over 5,000 acres.

Between 1730 and 1748, enough people had settled to establish Frederick County. By 1755, it had the highest population of any county in Maryland. The territory was soon being farmed by hardworking German immigrants who had left their homeland for greater freedom. Many came to escape religious persecution in Europe. Others came to join family members already in the New World. Many of them moved to the county from Pennsylvania, where they had originally settled. At first, German was spoken more than English. These Germans were the most successful of the settlers who came. They tanned leather and knitted long stockings for the farmers and frontiersmen. They also grew flax, which was spun and woven into linen. They were fortunate to have good soil, abundant water, and a mild climate. For recreation, they held barn raisings, quilting bees, corn-husking bees, and dances. The German settlers also had "schnitzing" bees, where apples were sliced and prepared for cooking. Early homes were log houses built near streams or springs.

The German settlers had few problems with the natives since they kept to themselves and showed the native people they wished to live peacefully with them.

Since many of the early farmers were German, the customs were primarily German. Throughout the county, German influence on architecture can be seen, especially in the city of Frederick where rows of old homes remain. These people lived a simple life, going to bed early and rising early. Families were large. Sons worked in the fields and daughters were expected to help their mothers. Markets were located far away and roads were exceptionally bad. Many things were made at home. The women spun wool into yarn, wove the yarn into fabric on handmade looms, then sewed the fabric into clothing for the entire family. They also grew a variety of crops, including tobacco, which was used as money.

Harford County began at the current site of Havre de Grace. Leonard Calvert, the Lord Proprietor, assigned some land in the area to a man named Godfrey Harmer in 1658. It became known as Harmer's Town, but Harmer did little to encourage people to settle there. In 1659, he assigned it to Thomas Stockett. The settlement then became Stockett's Town. For a while, fear of the Indians kept many people from settling. Then in 1661, Colonel Nathaniel Utie made a treaty with the Susquehannocks, and more settlers came. The settlement grew and was eventually bought by Jacob Looten, a fur trader.

According to the treaty, in order to distinguish the Susquehannocks from other Indians *FUN FACT* in the area, any Susquehannock who wanted to enter the settlement had to go first to the home of Captain Stockett or Jacob Clauson to get a ticket.

In 1695, two men, Jacob Young and William York, started a ferry service across the Susquehanna River near Stockett's Town. The settlement then became known as the Susquehanna Lower Ferry. There was an Upper Ferry, too, farther up the river near Lapidum. In 1782, the name Susquehanna Lower Ferry was changed to Havre de Grace. The Marquis de Lafayette, a French general who had played an important role in the American Revolution, had returned to America to visit General George Washington. When he saw the town and the beautiful surrounding area, he supposedly thought it looked like Le Havre de Grace, France. People in the settlement accepted the name, and it has since been known as Havre de Grace.

The land that would become **Carroll County** was first settled in 1723 by people who received land grants from Charles Calvert, the fifth Lord Baltimore. This was almost one hundred years after the first colonists began settling in Maryland.

FUN FACT   Some early land patents (a legal document granting ownership) with unusual names were Mulberry Bottom, Cranberry Plains, Buck Forest, Bellyache Thicket, Rattlesnake Ridge, Cat Tail Marsh, Wee Bit, and Swamp Miserable.

The Carroll County settlers were descended from people who had come to America from England, Scotland, and Ireland. These settlers moved into the area that was originally Baltimore County. Many were living in Annapolis and Baltimore. Between 1748 and 1756, a group of twenty-eight hundred Germans moved into northern Maryland from Pennsylvania. Other settlers from Pennsylvania were of Swiss, Irish, and Scottish descent. They built farms and established the towns of Taneytown in 1754 and Westminster in 1764. Many Europeans settled in the county because the climate and terrain reminded them of their homeland.

Carroll County's geography was a factor in its settlement. Its fertile soil and the many streams and creeks lured settlers looking for good farmland with a ready supply of water. Other natural resources (trees, stone, iron, clay, limestone, slate, and marble) influenced the location of towns and industries. Water resources still play an important role in the growth and development of Carroll County.

Homes

The first settlers built crude huts of tree branches and bark, much like those that the natives built. They lived in these until they could build houses. The first houses were made of logs. These were sturdy and, if well built, could stand for many years. Most settlers built one- or two-room homes with a loft for sleeping and storage. In the summer, people ate outside on tables and benches placed under shade trees. In winter, they boarded up the windows of their homes and used fireplaces to provide heat and light.

Building a home was a group project for Baltimore County settlers. First, land was cleared for the cabin and logs were cut. During the next few days, all the neighbors came and helped to build the cabin. When the house was finished, furniture was made for the family. Once the cabin was ready, a housewarming was held for all the neighbors who had helped. With music and dancing, this party lasted into the night. Then the family officially took possession of their new home.

FUN FACT

No nails were used in early log cabins or in their furniture. Instead, the logs were notched at the ends so they would fit together. Plates were also made of wood. Barns were built much larger than the houses because the settlers needed the room for their livestock and grain storage.

During the early 1700s, most homes were still single-story log houses, but some families began to build frame or stone houses. A few of these were two-story buildings that may have been enlarged with wings and porches. The way people lived was reflected in this change from frontier to farm life. During the mid- to late-1700s, some landowners began to build larger and more beautiful houses. Because of the risk of fire, the kitchen for a large house was often located in a separate building or as a separate room attached to the house. Fire was an ever-present danger because the fireplace was the only source of heat. Fireplaces were also used for cooking. There were no stores, so settlers hunted wild game and raised farm animals for meat and grew their own food.

FUN FACT

Food was cooked in kitchen fireplaces that were so big in many homes that a person could walk into them and stand upright.

Fire also provided light. The people used homemade candles and oil lamps. They also made their own clothes and soap. Life was hard. There was no modern farm equipment. Seeds were planted and crops were harvested by hand.

Water was clean and plentiful. There was no pollution then. The only problem was getting the water to the crops or into the house. The settlers used springs, and they dug wells. These wells were often at least fifty feet deep, and they were dug by hand. Water was hauled up in buckets. Around 1800, people started using large wooden pumps. Red Pump Road near Bel Air in Harford County got its name from a pump that was there.

FUN FACT	There was almost no money in the early colony. Even wealthy people often paid for things with tobacco, which was a very important crop and was protected by laws.

In Frederick County, early homes were log houses built near streams or springs. As people became wealthier, they built brick or stone homes. The colonists lived a pioneer life confronted by difficulties that included growing their own food and making their own clothing. They also faced dangers from wild animals. Few homes had books. The settlers passed Bibles from generation to generation, and family records were written in them.

In the early 1700s, homes were built from materials that were available. Foundations were constructed from stone. Logs were used for the walls, shingles for the roofs, and iron for the hardware. Bricks were made from local clay. In the late 1700s, in the area that would become Carroll County, farmers became more prosperous so they built larger, more fancy homes. By the 1800s, people quarried marble, slate, and limestone for building.

Establishment of the Boundary with Pennsylvania

For many years, there was no official boundary between Maryland and Pennsylvania. The two states disputed the location of this line. Two Englishmen, Charles Mason and Jeremiah Dixon, were hired to survey it. They worked from November 1763 to December 1767, surveying this boundary, which became known as the Mason-Dixon Line. They placed a stone marker at each mile along this line. A crownstone (a fancier marker) was set every fifth mile. It showed the coat of arms of William Penn on the Pennsylvania side and of Lord Baltimore on the Maryland side. There are still twenty-one of these boundary stones on the Carroll County line. Mason and Dixon also surveyed the line between Maryland and Delaware.

Early County Government

Until 1674, when a section of Baltimore County became Cecil County, Baltimore County covered all of northern Maryland. Political divisions were needed to make it easier to govern the county. The people used areas called "hundreds." In each area there lived approximately one hundred men who could be called for military duty. From these groups of men, the term hundred came into use and was used for over a hundred years. Dividing the county into hundreds made it easier to collect taxes and to count people for a census. In 1790, hundreds were replaced by election districts, which are still used today. Justices were replaced by commissioners to govern the county.

Early county government in Maryland was based on the English form of government. The court in each county was the center of government. Officers of the court were known by different names, such as justice, justice of the court, or commissioner, but the jobs were the same—to hold trials of people who broke laws and to levy taxes to pay for things such as road maintenance. Roads, ferries, and inns were under the control of the courts. Each had to be maintained to a certain standard. People were also paid by the county to serve on juries.

FUN FACT

One odd payment from county tax money was made for the killing of wild animals, particularly dangerous animals such as bears or wolves. This was meant to encourage people to kill the animals in order to make the area safer for the colonists. Squirrels were a nuisance, and were also killed for payment. Job Evans was paid forty-eight pounds of tobacco in 1737 for turning in twenty-four squirrel heads. William Rogers was paid one pound of tobacco the same year for a wolf's head. They were paid by the justices of the court.

When the courts convicted someone of a crime, the lawbreaker was often sentenced to jail for a certain period of time. Prisoners slept on straw beds in jails that had no heat for warmth in the winter. If someone committed a serious crime, he was put into leg irons. There were so few judges that cases couldn't be heard on a regular basis. Some prisoners spent so many years in jail that their clothing actually rotted to pieces. In addition, prisoners had to pay for their own imprisonment. If they could not pay, they sold themselves as servants for a period of time after their release and worked until they had paid off their debt.

Another very important official during early colonial times was the sheriff. He had a much wider variety of duties than sheriffs have today. Sheriffs had to keep the peace and arrest lawbreakers. They also had to select juries for trials, collect taxes from the colonists, advise the governor of events in the county, and hold elections when instructed to do so. The sheriff was also in charge of spreading the word about new laws that were passed. Usually he did this by posting notices of the new law in public places so people could read them. Since many people could not read, word of mouth was also an important way to spread the news.

Establishment of Towns

Baltimore County had few towns before 1715. Most people farmed. During the mid- and late-1700s, towns began to grow around taverns and country stores. People who did not want to farm or those who had a skill that was needed in the community moved into the towns. Hotels and shops that included blacksmiths and wheelwrights served the families of the area. There were many inns and taverns. Mills became an important source of jobs, and some towns grew up around mills.

One of Baltimore County's first important towns was called Joppa, then the county seat, located in what is now Harford County. Joppa was a busy tobacco port town established near the mouth of the Gunpowder River. By 1750, Joppa had a church, a courthouse (built in 1709), three warehouses, and a wharf, as well as several stores, inns, and taverns. It was a popular place to visit because horse races were held there.

During this time, colonists were also settling along the Patapsco River, and another port town was growing. Baltimore Town had a much better harbor than Joppa, and so it would grow much larger. Because of its nearness to the ironwork factories and mills, and because it had a harbor that could dock large ships, Baltimore Town became the economic center of Maryland in the late 1700s. People sent goods from all over the state to be shipped from Baltimore Town to markets in Europe and the Caribbean. During the late 1700s, Baltimore Town had a weekly newspaper, a theater, and two jewelry stores, things that other towns in northern Maryland did not have.

Many early towns like Harmer's Town (which became Havre de Grace in Harford County) grew up along the water. It was safer from Indians along the river, and transportation was much easier. Areas that had good natural harbors had the best chance of being settled. Later towns like Scott's Old Fields (which became Bel Air) were settled farther inland after the land was cleared and roads were built.

Quite a few gristmills (places to grind grain into flour) were built along streams in early northern Maryland. Many roads are named for them today. Most towns had warehouses to store goods until they could be sold and shipped.

Each of the towns in Frederick and Carroll counties most likely started with a tavern, store, inn, or mill along a public road. The settlers cleared land for farming. Some farmers had their land surveyed and sold the lots. The owner might declare a group of lots to be a town and give it a name. The first of these towns in Carroll County was Taneytown. Located between Frederick and York, Pennsylvania, it was laid out around 1754 by a member of the Taney family.

By the 1800s, a typical colonial town had a blacksmith and harness shop, one or more general stores, and a post office. There may have been churches, one or more inns, and a foundry where metal tools and hardware were made. Taverns continued to be popular meeting places. There would have been a need for a wagon wheel maker and a gristmill.

Establishment of Roads and Transportation

Early roads were narrow, winding paths, or faint trails formed by animals such as deer, elk, and bears. Settlers knew of these trails, but only a few well-experienced woodsmen could actually find them. The Indians also used these paths. They were usually located on high ridges, where water could drain off easily and snow would be blown away.

Early animal trails were only about 18 inches wide. Some well-known roads in Baltimore and Harford counties ran through the old wallowing spots (where the animals rolled in the mud) along the trails. They include Harford Road, Belair Road, Joppa Road, Old Court Road, and Old Philadelphia Road. Harford Road was once part of a turnpike (toll road where people pay to use the road) that ran from Baltimore Town to the Susquehanna River in Harford County.

FUN FACT

Transportation played a large role in the growth of towns and also in the wars that were to come. In 1666, a law was passed by the General Assembly ordering all counties to widen paths and build roads. First, roadways were widened so that horses and mules could travel over them. Then, they were improved so that wagons could use them. These roads were not paved, so they were often muddy and full of ruts. Most of the roads ran through thick forests. When the road reached a marsh, logs were laid side by side across the marshy area and covered with dirt. These were called corduroy roads, and they were terribly bumpy. Roads were so bad that a 10-mile trip from Baltimore to the Hampton Mansion in Towson could take from seven to nine hours.

A major north-south route from Alexandria, Virginia, to Philadelphia, Pennsylvania, ran through Baltimore County and what is now Harford County. There were no bridges at first. If travelers came to shallow water, they waded across. They took a ferry if one was available. In 1687, a more direct route was built.

FUN FACT	There were no road signs at the time. Travelers used notches on trees to point the way. Two notches marked a road leading to a courthouse or a church. Three notches marked a road leading to a ferry.

By this time, many people were traveling by stagecoach, which was a wagon with a wooden roof. There were three rows of seats inside. In the first row, the people rode sitting backwards, leaning against the front of the stagecoach. In the third row, they could lean against the back of the stage. However, those in the middle had nothing to lean on. Often luggage, mail bags, and sometimes even live chickens were at their feet.

FUN FACT	The first bridge built in Harford County was over the Gunpowder River in 1774. It was paid for with tobacco.

A team of horses pulled the stagecoach, and the horses were changed every ten miles at relay stations. Four horses pulling a stagecoach over poor roads could travel only about one mile per hour.

In the 1700s, more people moved into **Baltimore County.** There
was a need for better roads to transport tobacco, corn, and wheat to harbors and markets. Tobacco was packed in huge barrels called hogsheads. These were so big and heavy, they could not be moved by wagon
but had to be rolled along the roads by men or horses. These roads were
known as rolling roads. In Baltimore County, they extended to Elkridge
Landing and Joppa. Sections of Rolling Road, Old Court Road, Manor
Road, and Joppa Road used to be rolling roads.

In 1787, Baltimore County authorized the construction of turnpikes. They were nothing like today's turnpikes. They had toll gates every few miles. The gates blocked the road until the traveler paid the toll.

In the 1790s, a need for private turnpikes grew
because the public turnpikes were failures due to lack of
money for maintenance. In the 1800s, a corporation
could build a turnpike and charge a toll to those
using it. The Bel Air Turnpike, which was 2½ miles
long, extended from Bel Air to a site near Benson
and is now part of business Route 1.

During the 1800s, more roads and private turnpikes were built,
mainly to give easier access into Baltimore City and to the port. The
turnpikes were made of gravel, crushed stone, or other materials.

Because there were so few roads in the early 1700s, there were few settlers in southeastern **Frederick County.** In 1733, the first east-west road was recorded. This is important because at that time most roads in that area ran north and south. Most people of that time traveled by foot or by horse. An old Native American trail known as the Monocacy Trail started in Lancaster, Pennsylvania. It was the only road over which wagons could travel south to Frederick County. This trail had been cleared of brush as early as the 1740s. A road to Cumberland was cleared when General Edward Braddock marched to Fort Duquesne in Pennsylvania during the French and Indian War. This road later became part of the National Pike to the West.

If a road was well traveled, the court appointed an overseer whose job was to make sure that road was kept cleared and passable.

By 1799, stagecoaches were operating from Fredericktown to Baltimore, Hagerstown, and Georgetown in Maryland and to York and Lancaster in Pennsylvania. Fredericktown (later Frederick) became an important crossroads when the National Pike was finished in 1808 because it crossed another well-traveled road running from Harrisburg, Pennsylvania, to Washington.

FUN FACT	The stagecoach from Fredericktown to Georgetown left at 3:00 A.M. It reached Georgetown late in the evening. The fare was $3.00.

In **Harford County,** many roads were built leading out of Bel Air like the spokes of a wheel. The first macadam (broken stone) road was built from Bel Air to Churchville. Turnpikes were also built. People had to pay a toll of a few cents to use these.

Many of **Carroll County's** roads were originally Indian trails. Route 30 from Reisterstown to Hanover, Pennsylvania, was an Indian path that was eventually called the Conestoga Road. Another early Indian trail later called the Conestoga Wagon Road is Maryland Route 194 from Taneytown to Frederick.

In Carroll County, 42 miles of turnpike were built during the 1840s. By 1900, there were about 800 miles of roads in the county. With these improvements, farmers could more easily market their crops and move their equipment. The road that ran from Westminster to Reisterstown was 10 to 15 feet wide and was the most frequently used.

Many wooden bridges existed by this time. Those that were not covered with a roof became run-down. Some bridges were made of stone, but they were expensive to build and were often damaged by freezing water.

Another important means of travel throughout the area was by water. In 1784, Maryland and Virginia joined to establish the Potomac Company. Its purpose was to build a waterway to the west. It later became known as the Chesapeake and Ohio Canal Company. The C&O Canal ran from Washington, D.C., to Cumberland, Maryland, along the Potomac River. It has not been used since 1924 and is now a national historic park.

Railroads

Before the railroads, most travel was done by horse-drawn buggies, wagons, or stagecoaches. Road travel was dangerous, uncomfortable, and very slow. Robberies, overturned stages, and mud were constant problems. Railroads were an improvement for travel. At first, they were no safer or faster than roads, but the ride was smoother. The earliest railroad car was simply a wagon. Its wheels were placed on the rails, and it was pulled by a horse. Eventually, steam engines were invented, and railroads became a vital link between cities and states.

For **Baltimore County,** the most important development in transportation came with the building of the railroad. The first line was built from 1828 to 1830 by the Baltimore and Ohio Railroad (B&O). It ran between Baltimore and Ellicott's Mills. By horse and buggy, it had taken a full day to travel from Baltimore to Ellicott's Mills. By train, the trip took an hour. Since the horses pulling these early trains would tire before getting to Ellicott's Mills, a relay station was built. Here the teams of horses were changed. Today, the town of Relay marks the site of that station.

This early line of the Baltimore and Ohio Railroad was positioned in an east-west direction. A second railroad was planned to head north toward the Susquehanna River and into Pennsylvania. This second line was known as the Baltimore and Susquehanna Railroad. The Pennsylvania legislature refused to give the railroad the right to pass through the state, believing the state should profit from the railroad, not a private company. The owners of the rail line then stopped work on the line. There was a delay of several years before a line was built from Maryland into Pennsylvania.

FUN FACT	During the 1800s, railroad companies built recreation areas in the counties to encourage travel from the city. Baseball was also a popular reason for people to ride the train out to the rural areas. They could see games played by such teams as the Bears and the Bulls who played in Baltimore County. In May 1882, the score of one game was very high for baseball. The Bulls beat the Bears 45 to 42.

The railroad came to **Frederick County** in 1830. The Baltimore and Ohio Railroad built a line through Frederick Junction, about two miles south of the city of Frederick. People in Frederick did not want the railroad coming to their city. They were afraid it would bring too much growth, and they liked their town just the way it was.

Another line built by the Western Maryland Railroad in 1870 ran through what is now Thurmont (then known as Mechanicstown). In 1872, a branch line of the Pennsylvania Railroad came into Frederick.

Harford County's railroad line was located where the Amtrak line is today. It ran through the historic area from Joppa, through Bush, to Havre de Grace. It opened in 1836 and was called the Philadelphia, Wilmington, and Baltimore Railroad (PW&B). At the beginning, train cars were ferried across the river at Havre de Grace.

FUN FACT	The winter of 1852 was so cold that railroad officials were able to lay track across ice that was 2 to 3 feet thick on the Susquehanna River, then pull the train cars across the ice with horses.

In 1866, a bridge completed the link between Baltimore and Philadelphia. The PW&B was taken over by the Pennsylvania Railroad system in 1902. In 1908, a new railroad bridge was built and the old bridge was used as a highway bridge until 1939.

Another railroad in Harford County was the Ma and Pa Railroad, established in 1901 when other railroad companies joined. One of the earlier railroads, the Maryland Central, was planned in 1867. Portions of the route that became the Ma and Pa were built between 1873 and 1884. The Ma and Pa made its last run in Maryland in 1958.

Railroads in **Carroll County** were built before the county was officially established. Beginning in 1830, the Baltimore and Ohio Company built a railroad through the county. Eventually, it extended as far as Cumberland in Garrett County. By 1831, the line had reached Ridgeville, where there is a large hill called Parr's Ridge. It was hard for the trains to go over the hill, so to avoid Parr's Ridge, the railroad built the line through Mt. Airy. Later, in 1901, a tunnel was built through Parr's Ridge. It was the longest tunnel in the Baltimore and Ohio Railroad's system. This helped the growth of Ridgeville.

Division of Baltimore County

The original Baltimore County did not have established boundaries. This led to confusion at times, especially when property that was described and sold as part of Baltimore County was actually in Pennsylvania. The large area covered much of northeastern and central Maryland, including land on the Eastern Shore. The size of the county made it difficult for the leaders to govern it properly. It was decided to divide the area into separate counties because of its size as well as its growing population. Therefore, the history of early Baltimore County also tells the story of all northern Maryland.

The first county to separate from Baltimore County was Cecil County in 1674. Harford County withdrew in 1773. Carroll County was created in 1837, and Baltimore City separated in 1851. At the time, Baltimore City was the third largest city in the nation, and had governmental needs that were different from those of the county. Baltimore County then established Towson as its county seat.

REVOLUTIONARY TIMES

The French and Indian War

The French and Indian War was fought between the French and the British for domination in the New World. Each side had allies among the colonists and the Native Americans. A third group, consisting of the Iroquois tribes and known as the Iroquois Confederacy, was trying to preserve its freedom and its land in the Ohio Valley.

When the war began in 1755, Fredericktown was at the edge of the frontier. West of the city, Frederick County was wilderness, so the city became the major outpost where military plans and preparations were made.

In 1755, General Edward Braddock and 1,400 of his British troops marched into Fredericktown. George Washington, then a young colonel, came to Fredericktown at that time to help plan an attack on Fort Duquesne in Pennsylvania. Benjamin Franklin helped General Braddock get the wagons he desperately needed to carry food and other supplies west. General Braddock then headed west toward Fort

Duquesne, where a battle was fought. Braddock and his men were defeated at this battle. Braddock was injured, and he died three days afterward. Later, the British regained control of Fort Duquesne (renamed Fort Pitt) and other forts, eventually winning the war. The Treaty of Paris ended the French and Indian War in 1763.

Revolutionary War

Because of debt from the French and Indian War, England began to tax the American colonies on items such as tea and glass. Another of these taxes was imposed by the Stamp Act in 1765. All legal documents, newspapers, even dice and playing cards were required to have a stamp purchased with silver. For some time, colonists in America had been very angry with the English government. The colonists were not allowed to have representatives in Parliament (the English legislature, similar to the U.S. Congress) to look after their interests. They were being forced to pay unfair taxes. Colonists were especially upset about the tax on tea. In December of 1773, angry citizens boarded English ships in Boston Harbor and threw the cargo of tea overboard. England then punished the colonists for this "Boston Tea Party" by closing the harbor; no trade goods could be moved in or out.

On April 19, 1775, the British fought their first real battle against the patriots (colonists) at the Battle of Lexington and Concord. The Revolutionary War had begun.

Baltimore County was active in the rebellion before the war began. The merchants of the county agreed that they would not import goods from Britain. In November 1774, they established a Committee of Observation to enforce the agreement.

The colonists also started a Sons of Liberty organization. By 1776, Baltimore County was busy recruiting battalions of soldiers for defense against the British. They joined with men from other counties. During the war, Baltimore County supplied cannons and other needed items to the patriot army. These were made at an iron furnace at what is now the Loch Raven Reservoir. The county also provided much food, including flour that had been ground at its many mills.

There were several war heroes from the county. The best known is John Eager Howard, who was born in 1752 near what is now Pikesville. He served as a major in the Fourth Regiment of the Maryland Line.

Nathaniel Ramsey was also from Baltimore County and he became a colonel in the army. He and his men fought to save General George Washington's troops at a battle in Monmouth, New Jersey.

On November 23, 1775, the **Frederick County** Court officially repudiated the Stamp Act. This meant that the people had decided the Stamp Act was illegal and they would not purchase the stamps.

One week after Frederick County repudiated the Stamp Act, the town of Frederick buried it. A fake body was put into a coffin. The coffin was carried through town in a funeral parade by the Sons of Liberty and a military company and then buried.

FUN FACT

As more taxes were passed by the British government, Frederick County residents also became angry. After Boston Harbor was closed, a meeting was held in the Frederick County courthouse. The meeting was led by John Hanson. County residents favored stopping trade with the British. Soon after this meeting, they formed a militia for protection.

Prior to the Revolutionary War, Frederick County officials wrote a series of "resolves" declaring their loyalty to the king and reaffirming the Magna Carta, a document signed by King John of England in 1215, granting certain civil and political freedoms to the English people. In 1774, a new set of eight resolves was written after the residents' views had changed, and they wanted to be independent. These were similar to Harford County's Bush Resolutions, which are described later.

During the war, iron ore from Frederick County was used to make cannons. The Catoctin Furnace made cannonballs and kettles. These were used by General George Washington's army.

There were no battles fought in Frederick County during the war, but many men between the ages of sixteen and fifty fought in the Continental (colonial) Army.

The Bush Resolutions and Declaration

The town of Bush in **Harford County** was located on Old Philadelphia Road, the main highway going north and south. This was the road to Philadelphia, where the Continental Congress met. Many people wanted to be free from England and to rule themselves in America. George Washington, Thomas Jefferson, and other patriots passed through Bush on their way to the Congress in Philadelphia. Sometimes they stopped there, and people from the surrounding area met with them and discussed problems. When the British closed Boston Harbor, all the colonies felt they had to protest.

In 1774, the leaders of the new Harford County wrote a series of seven resolutions (statements of things they intended to do). These were presented to the General Assembly in Annapolis.

The first called for the colonies to unite and try to persuade England to reopen Boston Harbor. The second said that no one in Harford County would trade with Great Britain. The third stated that no trade other than rice would take place with the West India Islands, which were owned by Britain. The fourth resolution indicated Harford County would join with other colonies in sending relief to Boston, because the harbor had been closed by the British. The fifth said that merchants should not raise the prices of their goods. The sixth said that "gentlemen of the law" should "bring no suit for recovery of any debt due from any inhabitants of Great Britain," except in certain cases, until the crisis was over. The seventh stated that a committee of Harford gentlemen would meet with committees of other counties. They would try to work out ways to save constitutional rights, and "promote...union and harmony with Great Britain and her colonies."

These resolutions are important because they show that although the residents of Harford County were angry with England in early

1774, they were not yet ready to break away. Residents of the county also showed support for the activities of the Continental Congress.

Harford County had a war committee by June 1774. Its members conferred with other counties about plans for war. In December 1774, they decided to form militia companies. There were no battles fought in Harford County during the war, but some companies joined the Continental Army and fought in other places such as New York. Guns were manufactured in Harford County for use in the war. One manufacturer was Jerusalem Mill.

By 1775, many colonists had become more dissatisfied with English rule. England would not repeal (do away with) acts such as the Stamp Act. Again Bush (or Harford Town) hosted Washington, Jefferson, Franklin, and others who were working toward independence. The Continental Congress met in Philadelphia. One member of the Congress was William Paca, who was born in Abingdon.

Anger spread in Harford County, and thirty-four men met in Bush to write the Bush Declaration. These thirty-four men had been elected by the approximately ten thousand white men who lived in the county at the time. (Women and black people could not vote.) This document, together with the minutes of the meeting where it was written, clearly showed that Harford was ready to support Boston's opposition to England. This was March 22, 1775, sixteen months before the Philadelphia Declaration of Independence. The next day, Patrick Henry gave his famous "Give me liberty" speech. Less than a month later, American and British troops met at Lexington and Concord in the first battle of the war.

The Bush Declaration disappeared for a number of years. It was found in 1900 in the basement of the old building in Bush where court was held. Also found were the minutes of the meeting of March 22, 1774. The building was torn down soon after. The declaration is now in the care of the Historical Society of Harford County.   *FUN FACT*

The Marquis de Lafayette passed through Harford County on his way to Yorktown, where he helped defeat British General Cornwallis in the battle that ended the war. On the way south, Lafayette and his troops camped near what is now Darlington at the estate of Colonel James Rigbie. The men were cold, hungry, and badly clothed. Some deserted, but Lafayette convinced the others to go on. A historical marker in the area reads: "Had Lafayette failed in quelling the mutiny of his troops here on Friday, April 13, 1781, the Battle of Yorktown might never have been fought." If the Battle of Yorktown had not been fought, the war could have dragged on for many more months.

No citizens from **Carroll County** would have fought in the Revolutionary War since the county was not formed until 1837.

THE WAR OF 1812

One event preceding the War of 1812 was a trade dispute between England and France. This spread to the United States and eventually led to war between England and the United States. Another lesser-known reason was England's desire to protect its last remaining land in the New World—Canada. Therefore, the presence of the British in the Chesapeake Bay area was meant to draw American troops away from the Canadian border.

The British were kidnapping American men and forcing them to work on their ships. People in the western settlements of the United States were also angry with the British for encouraging the Indians to attack.

In **Baltimore County,** the Battle of North Point was fought on September 12, 1814. After burning sections of Washington, D.C., British troops under General Robert Ross landed at North Point at the mouth of the Patapsco River. They marched up North Point Road toward Baltimore and were met by a troop of Americans who killed General Ross.

One of the most famous battles in American history then took place in the waters off Baltimore. British ships fired on Fort McHenry, but were not successful in their attempt to take Baltimore. Francis Scott Key wrote the poem the "Star-Spangled Banner" while watching the battle from a flag-of-truce vessel owned by a Baltimore ship owner. The poem became America's National Anthem.

Nathan Towson fought in the War of 1812. Nathan was a member of the family for whom the town of Towson was named. He served as a captain of the Baltimore County company that fought for possession of Canada. Known for its fierce fighting, his regiment was called "Lightning" by the British.

Frederick County saw no battles during the War of 1812, though many men from the area fought in the war. Fredericktown was used by the United States government as a safe place to store important documents during the war. British prisoners were brought from Washington and kept in the Fredericktown jail.

In **Harford County,** Havre de Grace suffered great damage during the War of 1812. The British had blockaded parts of the Chesapeake Bay, and their ships were attacking towns along its shores. Just before dawn on May 2, 1813, they attacked Havre de Grace. The British fired cannons at the town. Then they came ashore and started burning the buildings and stealing people's belongings. The town was almost completely destroyed by fire. John O'Neill was a hero in the attack on Havre de Grace. He single-handedly manned a cannon and fired on the British from a hill overlooking the town. After being injured by the recoil of the cannon, he went down into the town and was arrested by the British. He was held aboard one of the British barges for three days. Fearing for her father's life, his sixteen-year-old daughter Matilda rowed out to the ship and pleaded with the British admiral not to kill him. The admiral let him go. O'Neill later became the lighthouse keeper at the Concord Lighthouse in Havre de Grace when it was built in 1829.

Another hero in the war of 1812 was Commodore John Rodgers from Havre de Grace. He was patrolling the waters off the coast of Virginia in May 1812. A British ship fired on his ship. He ordered his men to fire back. This event took place before the war had started and contributed to the outbreak of the war. The following year, Rodgers saved

Baltimore from an attack by sinking the British ships in the channel so they could not reach the city. Commodore Rodgers received many honors for his successes during the war.

Carroll County had not been established during the time of this war, but people who lived in the area did participate.

After Matilda O'Neill had rowed out to the British ship to ask for her father's release, she was supposedly given a snuffbox (a box to hold tobacco) by the British admiral, who admired her courage. A sword was given to her father by the city of Philadelphia.

FUN FACT

SLAVERY, THE CIVIL WAR, AND EVENTS THAT FOLLOWED

Slavery

Slavery existed in **Baltimore County** in the 1700s and 1800s until 1864, when the newly adopted State Constitution of Maryland freed all the Maryland slaves. Citizens of Baltimore County were divided about the slavery issue. To the north was Pennsylvania, which was a free state for black people. To the south were Maryland counties that depended on slaves for their tobacco and other farming industries. Baltimore County had large farms, but it also had industries such as iron furnaces, paper mills, and grain mills, which used slave labor. In earlier years, when tobacco was the main crop, Baltimore County residents used slaves to plant, grow, and harvest the tobacco. But after the Revolutionary War, antislavery movements grew. An organization called the Maryland State Colonization Society was formed in 1831 in Baltimore City. Its aim was to help slaves and free blacks who wanted to go back to Africa. By 1840, the organization had helped 624 people return to Africa and establish a colony there in the country of Liberia. The colony was known as Maryland in Liberia. The society ran low on money but continued to send people to Africa, though at a slower rate.

British landowners brought many of the first slaves to plantations in southern and eastern **Frederick County,** where slaves were treated differently depending on their owners. They worked on farms planting and harvesting crops such as wheat. By 1860, just before the Civil War, there were 3,243 slaves and 4,967 free blacks. These freedmen had fewer rights than whites. By law, black people were not allowed to hold meetings at night or to be out after 10:00 P.M. Several former slave quarters are still in existence today. One is located at 114 West Second Street behind the Ross-Mathias Mansion. Another, at 121 South Benz Street in Frederick, was once owned by Chief Justice Roger B. Taney.

Harford County was a slave county within a slave state. Most of the slaves lived in the southern part of the county. In the 1600s, some worked in the fields growing tobacco and other crops. Others worked in the iron forges. Some worked in the house as maids, cooks, and nannies. Blacksmithing, stone masonry, or other skilled labor was taught to them. Some worked in town shops. By the 1700s, most were owned by small farmers. Others were sold for cash and sent to the South. Slaves had a better life in Maryland than in the Deep South because they worked directly for their owners. During the years leading up to the Civil War, many people realized that slavery should be abolished. By the time of the Civil War, some slaves in the county had been freed by their owners and were known as freedmen and freedwomen. The census of 1860 reports 1,800 slaves in Harford County and 3,644 freedmen and freedwomen.

In **Carroll County,** people were divided about slavery. Before the Civil War, two-thirds of the county's slaves lived in the southern part of the county. There were fewer slaves in the north because they were not needed on the small German farms or in the craft businesses in the towns. Carroll County's slaves worked mainly on tobacco plantations. Some worked as housekeepers. According to the 1837 assessment of property, there were 1,044 slaves in Carroll County's nine largest towns and their total value was $220,400. Because of religious groups such as the Quakers, who were opposed to slavery, about half the black people in Carroll were free blacks and half were slaves. Cultural groups differed in how they felt about slavery. The Germans in the North did not believe in slavery; the English in the southern area did.

Underground Railroad

The Underground Railroad did not run on rails and had no engine or caboose. But it did have conductors and stations. The conductors helped runaway slaves from the South find freedom in the North. These people were called "abolitionists" because they knew slavery was wrong, and they wanted it abolished (stopped).

Before 1850, slaves who had escaped could receive help getting to Baltimore City or Pennsylvania. The city was a major stop for those escaping north on the railroads. Some people in **Baltimore County** helped, though the Underground Railroad system was not very extensive there.

The Baltimore and Susquehanna Railroad officially maintained a policy of providing boxcars to return runaway slaves. But some people along the route helped the slaves on their journey north. Several sites along the Baltimore and Susquehanna and the Northern Central Railroad routes have been described as stations on the Underground Railroad, but this has not been verified. Sometimes, abolitionists would tell stories that made it seem as though slavery was on its way out.

In 1850, the Fugitive Slave Act was passed by the United States Congress. It gave stricter sentences to people caught helping slaves escape. They could be sent to jail or fined up to $1,000. After the passage of this law, Baltimore County residents did very little to help slaves.

After slave owner Edward Gorsuch from Monkton was killed in Christiana, Pennsylvania, trying to get his slaves back, white people were even less sympathetic to the slaves' cause. Gorsuch was widely known as a "kind owner," and people were outraged and frightened by his murder. This incident became known as the Christiana Riot.

Little if any Underground Railroad activity took place in either **Frederick County** or **Carroll County.** There are some cases from the 1850s that describe runaway slaves who had been caught. They were lodged in the county jail. There are also some references to safe houses—places where slaves could hide.

In northern **Harford County,** where there were many Quakers, the abolitionists had a network of hiding places or "stations." The slaves were smuggled along secret routes from station to station. Since Underground Railroad stations were secret places, it is hard to locate them today. Three have been found in Harford County. One is Swallow Fields, a house that was owned by Quakers named Waring. They hid the slaves in their home or in an icehouse until it was safe for them to be taken across the Susquehanna River. Another was the property of a family named Worthington, who lived near Darlington. Both of these sites were in the northern part of the county, close to the river and to freedom. Pennsylvania was considered "freedom" because slavery had been abolished there in 1780. The third station was the house of a black man named Richard Harris. He was the man who rowed the slaves across the Susquehanna River to Cecil County, a short distance from the Pennsylvania border. His house was just north of the place where the Conowingo Dam is now located. The site was covered by the lake created by this dam, so it is no longer visible.

FUN FACT

Conductors on the Underground Railroad used code words to tell each other when slaves were on the way. Supposedly, when a Quaker conductor told his servants to "kill a sheep," that meant slaves were expected soon and would need to be ferried across the river.

The Civil War

At the time of the Civil War, farms in **Baltimore County** were small and were worked by the farmer, his family, and sometimes a few hired workers. As manufacturing became important, factory owners needed skilled labor, not slave labor. By the start of the Civil War, there were few slaves in Baltimore County.

FUN FACT

Just before the war, a presidential election was held. Four men were running: Stephen A. Douglas, John Bell, John C. Breckinridge, and Abraham Lincoln. Lincoln won the election, but he was not at all popular in Baltimore County. He received only thirty-seven votes.

After the election, Southern states began to secede (declare that they were no longer part of the United States). Along with the slavery issue, there were economic reasons for this, as well as differences in lifestyle and thinking. The Civil War began on April 12, 1861, when Southern troops (Confederates) fired on Fort Sumter at Charleston, South Carolina. The fort was federal property, and President Lincoln and the Northern (Union) states did not want the Confederacy to have it. The war would divide families as well as the nation.

Baltimore City had a large number of Confederate sympathizers. It was also the hub of the railroads. The first skirmish of the Civil War in Maryland happened in Baltimore. On April 19, 1861, a train carrying Northern militiamen from the Sixth Massachusetts Regiment pulled into the President Street Station. After the soldiers got off the train, they were attacked by angry pro-Confederates. Captain Albert S. Follansbee, the leader of the Massachusetts regiment, commanded his men to fire. Eight Southern sympathizers, two militiamen, and one innocent bystander were killed.

For the most part, people from Baltimore County sided with the North before and during the war. Prior to the war, meetings were held throughout the county to discuss the issues. People did not want to secede from the Union, but they also did not want war to force the South to stay in the Union. They were afraid that newly elected President Lincoln would be unable to hold the country together.

FUN FACT   The county could not raise enough volunteer soldiers to meet Union quotas. Some men "hired" other men to fight for them, paying $300 to $700 for these substitutes. Though notices appeared in the *Baltimore County American* newspaper, not enough men responded. More black men than white men responded.

President Lincoln was concerned that Maryland was going to join the Confederacy, so he called for the arrest of people who were supporting the South. During the Civil War, Baltimore County and many other sections of Maryland were put under martial law (the military was in charge).

The railroad was a vital link between the North and the South. In Maryland, the B&O, the Philadelphia, Wilmington, and Baltimore, and the Northern Central were closely guarded by Union troops. Soldiers and supplies were transported on all the lines. The B&O line between Baltimore and Washington was particularly important, as was the Thomas Viaduct across the Patapsco River. This viaduct carried not only the railroad tracks, but also telegraph lines.

Even though there were a few scares during the war, no significant battles were fought in Baltimore County. One such scare was in July 1864, when Confederate troops under General Bradley T. Johnson came through the county.

FUN FACT

When Johnson's troops rode into Owings Mills, they seized a shipment of ice cream that was supposed to go to Baltimore. Many of the soldiers had never seen ice cream before. They thought it was frozen beer. Some soldiers put it into their canteens to melt. Some put it into their hats and ate it as they rode along.

People in **Frederick County** were torn between the Union and Confederate causes. Although many sympathized with the South, they did not want the nation divided into two countries. Most citizens became Union supporters. Some men from Frederick County joined the Confederate Army and some joined the Union Army. During the Battle of Gettysburg (the decisive battle of the war), these units fought each other at Culp's Hill.

Barbara Hauer Fritchie from Frederick County became famous because of a poem written by John Greenleaf Whittier about an incident he said happened in Frederick during the Civil War. On September 10, 1862, Confederate troops marched into the city of Frederick. Ninety-five-year-old Barbara Fritchie was a strong Union supporter. In the poem, as the troops marched past her house, she supposedly leaned out of an attic window and bravely waved the American flag. The troops fired at the flag, breaking the flag staff, but Fritchie continued waving it. This story is not true. The troops did not march past this house; they were a block away. Earlier in the year, Fritchie chased Confederate soldiers from her front steps, and other women did wave flags patriotically during the march through Frederick. Whittier, the famous American poet, heard about these incidents and wrote a poem about them. Using poetic license (when a writer breaks standard writing rules or changes facts to suit his creativity), he combined the incidents and called his poem "Barbara Fritchie." The poem was published in the *Atlantic Monthly* in October 1863. Long after her death at age ninety-six, Fritchie's house was destroyed by a flood. A replica was built in the 1920s.

FUN FACT   On December 17, 1860, a county convention was held to determine how people felt about the issue of secession (withdrawing as a state of the United States). There was so much yelling that a voice vote was not possible. The people were told to "vote" by choosing one of two gates to leave the courthouse. Union supporters were to leave through the east gate; those who wanted Maryland to secede would leave from the south gate. Nearly three times as many people left through the east gate, so Frederick voted for Maryland to remain part of the United States.

After marching through Frederick, the Confederate troops separated into two groups. General Stonewall Jackson and his men confronted the Union garrison at the strategic site of Harpers Ferry, West Virginia. At the same time, General Robert E. Lee and his men fought the Union troops of General George McClellan at the Battle of South Mountain. Lee was forced to retreat to Antietam, where Jackson and his men rejoined him. On September 17, 1862, the Confederates faced McClellan at the Battle of Antietam, and Lee's invasion was stopped. This has been called one of the bloodiest battles of the war. The total of twenty-three thousand dead and wounded was almost evenly divided between North and South. Many of the wounded were brought to Frederick.

Churches and schools in Middletown and Frederick were quickly turned into hospitals. At this time, there were twenty hospitals in Frederick. They served over four thousand meals every day. The hospitals in Frederick also cared for wounded from the Battle of Gettysburg in 1863.

One of the men wounded at the Battle of South Mountain was Rutherford B. Hayes, who later became president of the United States.

President Lincoln stopped in Frederick on October 4, 1862, to tour Antietam after that bloody battle. He visited a wounded officer he knew and made a speech at the Frederick railroad station. He was warmly welcomed by the people in Frederick.

West of Frederick, the towns of Middletown and Boonsboro were the scenes of several skirmishes during the Civil War. After the battles of South Mountain and Antietam, many people who lived in these towns took wounded soldiers into their homes and cared for them. Churches were used as hospitals in these towns also. Middletown was occupied by Confederate forces twice during the war. The first was during the Battle of South Mountain. The second occupation in 1864 was by General Jubal Early on his way to Washington. While in Middletown, Early demanded five thousand dollars from the town or it would be burned. He settled for fifteen hundred dollars.

Middletown had its own "Barbara Fritchie." A seventeen-year-old girl named Nancy Crouse hung a flag from the second-story window of her house on West Main Street. A dozen Confederate cavalrymen on their way west entered the house. Nancy removed the flag from the window and wrapped it around herself. One cavalryman put a gun to her head and demanded the flag. At first, Nancy refused, but finally, she did give him the flag. That cavalryman tied the flag around his horse's head, and the men left town. A group of Union cavalrymen then chased and captured the Confederates. The flag was recovered and returned to Nancy Crouse.

FUN FACT

In July 1864, Confederate General Jubal Early marched into Frederick with his troops. He demanded that the city pay two hundred thousand dollars, or the city would be looted and burned. Mayor Cole and several banks in the city raised the money and took it to General Early. The general left with his men and marched south, hoping to seize the city of Washington. When they reached the Monocacy River, they found Union troops waiting for them. That day, 398 men died in the Battle of the Monocacy. Even though the Union troops lost, this battle was important because it delayed General Early and allowed Union forces to fortify Washington and protect it from Early and other Confederate troops.

Harford County reflected the whole country's concerns about the Civil War. It was divided, as was the country. The county was occupied by Union forces.

In Harford County, the Philadelphia, Wilmington, and Baltimore Railroad was very important to the Union for troop movement and for shipment of supplies. The fear was that Southern forces would destroy the tracks or blow up the railroad bridges. Union troops patrolled the tracks and bridges to defend them from the Confederates. In one raid, Confederates were able to destroy part of the railroad bridge over the Gunpowder River. In July 1864, Major Harry Gilmor led his band of Confederate troops into Harford County. They set two trains on fire and destroyed part of the bridge. Next, they raided the station at Gunpowder Neck and took five Union prisoners. Then they left the county, heading for western Maryland.

Although no battles were fought in Harford County, there were skirmishes. Small battles were fought between Northern and Southern troops over control of the covered bridge at Conowingo, which crossed the Susquehanna River.

| FUN FACT | Harford County had many incidents of barn-burnings. People favoring the South were accused of burning barns belonging to families favoring the North. Anyone who favored the South and lived within 6 miles of a barn-burning was fined. Many innocent people probably paid fines for these acts. |

People from Harford County fought on both sides of the war. Colonel Edwin H. Webster (Union Army) organized the Seventh Maryland Regiment, which included two companies of soldiers from Harford County, and served as its first commander. Many men from Harford County joined the Confederate States of America units from Virginia.

Brigadier General James J. Archer (Confederate Army) was commander of a brigade of men from Tennessee and Texas. He fought in the battles of Mechanicsville, Cold Harbor, Antietam, Chancellorsville, and the Battle of Gettysburg, where he was injured and taken prisoner.

Most people in **Carroll County** were Union sympathizers, though the majority did not vote for Abraham Lincoln in the 1860 election. In May 1861, Carroll County citizens passed a Declaration of Resolutions, stating they would resist efforts to include Maryland with the South. This was a reflection of their attitude toward slavery.

In 1860 and 1861, guard units were formed because townspeople were worried that war might come. These units were Southern sympathizers. Another group, the Carroll Infantry, was commanded by Captain George Wampler. Many members of this group joined the Union Army.

Because of its good roads, railroads, and location near Washington, D.C., the Carroll County area drew both Union and Confederate troops. In 1863, Major General J.E.B. Stuart and his Confederate troops had small skirmishes with citizens and Union troops on their way through the county toward Gettysburg. One such skirmish with Captain Charles Corbit's Union cavalry took place in downtown Westminster. The Confederate troops destroyed telegraph lines and sections of the B&O Railroad tracks. They burned bridges and wrecked the Howard Cotton Factory.

As they destroyed the cotton factory, Confederate soldiers took belts from the machinery to repair the soles of their boots.   *FUN FACT*

Just before the Battle of Gettysburg, Major Stuart's men fought a small troop of men from Delaware. This battle delayed Stuart's arrival in Gettysburg, so he was too late to help the Confederate cause there.

The booming sounds from the cannons at the Battle of Gettysburg could be heard in Taneytown, a distance of about 12 miles.   *FUN FACT*

Maryland's Civil War Governor

Maryland's governor during the Civil War was Augustus Bradford, who was born and raised in Bel Air in Harford County. He ran for governor as a representative of the Union Party and was elected on November 6, 1861. He was governor throughout the war. Bradford supported the North and was in favor of preserving the union of the United States. His election was contested by members of the pro-Confederate Peace Party. They said that the Union Party gave soldiers leave to return home to vote, thereby adding extra votes. They also accused the Union Party of allowing men who did not live in Maryland to vote.

NOT-SO-FUN FACT	Anger and distrust of Governor Bradford remained after the election was over. In 1864, a group of Confederate raiders burned the governor's home on Charles Street in Baltimore to show their feelings about the man and the election.

John Wilkes Booth

Without question, John Wilkes Booth is Harford County's most infamous historical figure. He was born near Bel Air in 1838. The house is called Tudor Hall. When Booth shot President Abraham Lincoln at Ford's Theater on April 14, 1865, the house was rented and the Booth family was not living there. John Wilkes Booth had attended schools in Bel Air, Baltimore, Catonsville, and York, Pennsylvania. However, he was not very interested in school. Booth was a fanatic Confederate sympathizer. He had originally intended to kidnap the president, but the South surrendered before that plot could be carried out. So Booth and several others formed another plan to kill several members of the government that night. They wanted to kill the president, the vice president, the secretary of state, and General Ulysses Grant. President Lincoln was the only one to die as a result of this plot. A cavalry troop cornered Booth with another conspirator in a Virginia tobacco barn two weeks later and killed him.

After the War

When the Civil War was over, there was still tension between people who had fought on opposite sides. People were bitter about arrests made during the war, as well as the harassment they had endured from the other side.

Some historians wonder if the man killed at the tobacco barn was really Booth. Years after the assassination (murder of a political figure), a mysterious mummy was shown in a circus and described as the body of John Wilkes Booth. The man had committed suicide in Enid, Oklahoma, in 1903, after telling several people over the years that he was Booth and that he had murdered the president. Did Booth escape and die years later by his own hand? In May of 1995, the descendants of the Booth family asked a court in Baltimore for permission to exhume John's body in Greenmount Cemetery and have it tested for identification. Their request was denied. During World War II, the mummy disappeared and has not been seen since, so the mystery remains.

Much property had been taken away. Some people had a difficult time adjusting to the newly gained freedom of black Americans. The Thirteenth Amendment abolished slavery in 1865, but race relations were particularly bad during the time of 1865 to 1870. Black people did not have the right to vote or to testify in court cases involving whites. Also, they did not enjoy other legal rights or social privileges that white people did. Tension between the races increased.

In 1867, the state of Maryland granted black people the right to vote and to attend public schools. This was before amendments to the U.S. Constitution granted these rights across the nation. In 1868, the Fourteenth Amendment gave black people citizenship and equal protection under the law. In 1870, the Fifteenth Amendment gave them the right to vote.

Transportation was improved during this time by streetcars—horse-drawn cars similar to railroad cars, but much smaller. These moved on tracks, or rails. Streetcar lines were a big improvement over roads, most of which were still unpaved. Many turnpikes were still in poor condition. With this quicker way to and from the city, people began moving to the suburbs and riding streetcars to jobs in the city.

In the late 1800s, the U.S. Congress decided to build forts along the coast to protect Baltimore City from attack. Fort Howard, Fort Smallwood, and Fort Armistead were built at this time. No battles were ever fought at these forts.

After the Civil War, many people in **Frederick County** were out of work due to the automation of factories. Machines were doing jobs formerly done by people. A committee of citizens began a campaign to urge the federal government to repay the two-hundred-thousand-dollar ransom that had been paid to General Jubal Early during the war. This campaign continued until 1886; however, it was the city (not the federal government) that repaid the banks in 1951.

During the 1880s, many immigrants moved to Frederick County. Most of them came from eastern European countries. Telephone service began in 1883, and electricity came to Frederick in 1887. New businesses opened such as the Frederick Seamless Hosiery Company and C.E. Cline's Carpets and Furniture.

Black-owned businesses opened on All Saints Street in Frederick. In the early 1900s, the first hospital for black people in Frederick opened its doors in what is now the Elks Lodge. It was opened by the first black doctors, Dr. Ullyses G. Bourne, Sr., and Dr. Charles Brooks.

After the war, people in **Harford County** started rebuilding their lives, too. They had to face their sadness over the loss of the president and loved ones who had been killed in the war. The next fifty years brought growth and progress to the county. Agriculture and canning were important industries in Harford County as was the mining of chrome, lime, iron, slate, flint, and marble. During this time, the dairy industry also grew in the county.

Following the Civil War, **Carroll County** saw a number of changes. In response to state law, the Carroll County School Commissioners were organized, creating a uniform school system in the county. The economy improved steadily. Developments included agricultural advances, gas-lighted streets, new factories, and telephones. The steady development of towns, businesses, small manufacturing companies, and farming helped to promote economic growth in the county.

The Western Maryland Railroad was extended in 1862 from Westminster to Union Bridge. The telegraph line that ran along the railroad was begun in 1862 and finished in 1864. Four years later, a line was opened from Union Bridge to Double Pipe Creek, which was later called Detour. This line, the Western Maryland Railroad, was established and paid for almost completely by Carroll County citizens.

On December 20, 1899, Carroll County became the first county in the United States to have countywide rural free mail delivery. The post office and distribution center for the mail was in Westminster.

FUN FACT

THE EARLY TWENTIETH CENTURY

In the late 1800s and early 1900s, immigrants from England, Ireland, and Germany arrived in northern Maryland. Others came from eastern and southern European countries such as Poland, Czechoslovakia, and Italy.

The early 1900s have been called the Progressive Era. Americans were seeking new laws to improve working conditions, hours, salaries, and safety for industrial workers. Women formed civic leagues to improve sanitary conditions in the towns and to promote proper behavior among their citizens.

During this early part of the century, the counties began to provide their citizens with more services. These included garbage disposal, sewage systems, street cleaning, electricity, and telephone service. Local police forces and fire departments were established.

Movies became popular, as did dance bands. Sports such as baseball, tennis, football, basketball, and bowling also became very popular.

Many people thought that drinking alcohol was wrong. Groups called temperance unions were formed to encourage people not to drink. In January 1920, the Eighteenth Amendment to the Constitution, called the Prohibition Amendment, went into effect. At this time, the sale of alcohol was against the law. (This law was repealed in 1933 by the Twenty-first Amendment.) Carroll County, however, had prohibited most alcohol since 1915. Their law was not as strict as the federal law. People were allowed to bring one gallon of liquor into the county each month.

In 1920, the Nineteenth Amendment gave women the right to vote.

Transportation

Dirt roads could still be found in the early 1900s. In bad weather, the new "horseless carriages" (cars) often became stuck in the mud. Horses or oxen pulled them out. Early cars did not have headlights. Drivers hung kerosene lamps near the roof of their cars to help them see at night.

Problems with the turnpikes continued into the early twentieth century. United Railway owned the three longest turnpikes—Harford, Belair, and York. In addition, they operated most of **Baltimore County**'s streetcars. It was believed that they were neglecting the roads purposely, hoping that people would use the streetcars.

All the counties were providing more money to improve roads, so these were in far better condition than the privately owned turnpikes. People questioned why they should pay to travel on a poorly kept turnpike when the county roads were so much better. Turnpikes were gradually sold. Most were bought by the State Roads Commission. The end of these early turnpikes brought about the modern age of travel, as automobiles replaced horse-drawn wagons and buggies.

Baltimore County was the leader in road improvement at this time because it was the first county to hire a road engineer. It was also the first county to use steam rollers on the road.

FUN FACT

In **Frederick County** at the turn of the century, trolleys became the newest means of transportation. A trolley was a streetcar with a pole on top that was connected to an overhead electric wire, which provided power. The trolley system was called the Frederick and Middletown

Passenger Railroad. It ran east and west from Frederick to Middletown. It carried freight as well as passengers, traveling about 20 miles per hour. The trolley line merged with other companies and changed names several times over the years. These companies owned their own electric power plants. Eventually, through the joining of companies, the Potomac Edison Company was established.

The trolleys lasted until the late 1930s. Many people had automobiles by that time. The trolley was used again briefly during World War II, because automobiles as well as gasoline and tires were scarce. In Frederick County, the trolley made its final trip in 1954.

Frederick's first bus service was started by the Blue Ridge Lines in the 1920s.

Until 1908, there was no bridge over the Susquehanna River for horses or cars. In that year, the Pennsylvania Railroad stopped using its bridge over the river. Seven people from **Harford** and Cecil counties bought the bridge for seven hundred dollars and converted it to a road bridge. They charged a toll. The bridge was used until 1928, when it was bought by the state and made into a double-deck bridge. In 1939, it was replaced by the present Thomas J. Hatem Memorial Bridge.

By 1900, there were about 800 miles of roads in **Carroll County.** Thirty miles of these roads were turnpikes. New bridges were built and older ones repaired. A covered bridge over the Monocacy River at Bridgeport was used until 1932.

Rail travel was also important in Carroll County in the early twentieth century. People could go to Baltimore in just a few hours. The

Western Maryland Railway had its general offices in the station at Union Bridge. It is now a museum.

When automobiles were invented, rail use in Carroll County dropped. Bus service was started between Westminster and Reisterstown around 1914. The Blue Ridge Bus Line carried passengers from Westminster to Baltimore in the 1930s.

World War I

The United States entered World War I in 1917, after the sinking of many U.S. merchant ships by the Germans. American troops were sent to Europe to help the Allied forces fighting against Germany and the other Central Powers. Women played a big role on the home front during World War I. Maryland Governor Harrington formed councils in each county to oversee war preparation and food conservation. Women served on these councils and joined the Red Cross, sometimes serving in Europe. Some women collected old clothes for European refugees.

People in **Baltimore County** feared war was coming before it was declared. They began forming national defense companies of volunteers. Many men did not want to go to war, so enrollment in the army was slow. In June 1917, the army started drafting men (calling them for their required military service). Once the war started, many went to war or took high-paying jobs in war-related industries. This left a shortage of farm workers, and production of food became a problem.

Children who were members of Boy Scout and Girl Scout troops were asked to work in gardens and on farms to grow more food. Nine Girl Scout troops were formed. They grew "victory gardens" to increase the production of food. Girl Scouts also helped by knitting warm clothes for soldiers, buying thrift stamps, and performing Red Cross work.

FUN FACT

During World War I, many men from **Frederick County** joined the 115th Infantry of the 29th Division organized at Camp McClellan in Alabama in October 1917. They suffered great losses; 25 percent of the 115th Infantry troops were killed or wounded. By the end of the war, twenty-six Frederick County men had been killed in action, seven died of wounds, one died at sea, forty died of disease, and five were declared MIA (missing in action).

When word reached Frederick that a peace treaty had been signed, hundreds of people celebrated in the streets. Whistles blew and bells rang to let everyone know the war was over. On November 18, 1918, a formal peace celebration featured an air show.

In **Harford County** the Jackson Guards were organized in 1887. They became part of the First Maryland Regiment National Guard in January 1888. They were pressed into service on August 5, 1917. Eleven hundred soldiers served in all branches of the military. Forty-five men died, most from diseases such as measles and the flu. They are remembered today with a memorial plaque attached to a stone marker located in Bel Air. The memorial was dedicated in 1923.

In Havre de Grace, older men organized a company of Home Guards. Women worked for the Red Cross. Many people bought Victory Bonds, which helped the U.S. government pay for our part in the war. The Aberdeen Proving Ground and Edgewood Arsenal were opened in Harford County. The army base developed and tested various types of weapons, including chemical weapons.

Carroll County's Council of Defense was part of the national and state Councils of Defense. The Maryland Assembly passed an act requiring all men over sixteen to register for the military. Approximately twelve hundred men and women from Carroll County joined the armed forces to serve during the war.

FUN FACT   Those who registered for the military were asked such questions as these: Can you ride a horse? Can you handle a team of horses? Can you operate a wireless radio? Do you have any experience with steam engines, electrical machinery, or high-speed boats with gasoline engines?

Because of the number of German descendants in Carroll County, some pro-German demonstrations were held during the war. Several German people received letters of censure from the Council of Defense, telling them of the penalties that would be given for anti-American expressions.

Local canners and farmers contributed to the war effort and also benefited from the war due to the large demand for canned goods overseas. Since many men were away fighting, the remaining farmers, including women and children, had to work longer hours to harvest the crops.

Children collected peach stones, which were used to make the carbon filters for gas masks used in Europe. (A gas mask is worn over the face to filter air and prevent the breathing of poisonous gases.) Two hundred peach stones were needed to make enough carbon for just one gas mask. *FUN FACT*

World War II

The United States entered World War II in 1941 following Japan's attack on Pearl Harbor, an American naval base in Hawaii. America had supported the Allied effort in Europe for three years, but U.S. troops were not involved until the Japanese attack. After World War II was declared, people started calling the 1914–1918 war World War I. (Between the two world wars, Germany had once again tried to take over countries in Europe, and Japan had become aggressive in the Pacific.)

Once World War II started, many things that are taken for granted today were in very short supply, such as tires, food, and appliances. Gasoline and fuel oil were rationed (people could buy only small amounts) because they were needed for war equipment. Many people ran out of oil to heat their homes. Metal was also needed. Many housewives donated aluminum cooking pots and other metal household items to be melted down and made into weapons. In **Baltimore County,** the Glenn L. Martin plant (which built military airplanes) designed a new bomber called the Flying Torpedo. Many important industries were located in Baltimore City and Baltimore County. It was feared that these industries would be a target for air raids.

The Red Cross is a relief organization that helps people in times of war, floods, and other emergencies. The Red Cross was active in the county, packing kits to be sent to the soldiers overseas. The kits contained soap, razor blades, playing cards, and chewing gum.

During World War II, men from **Frederick County** again served their country both in Europe and Asia. Company A of the 115th Regiment was among the first to land at Normandy, the site of a crucial battle in the war. Many people who did not serve overseas still worked for the war effort. Some worked at the shipyards and aircraft facilities in the Baltimore area. Frederick County organized a Civilian Defense Council on December 8, 1941. The organization had a fire chief, police chief, and air raid warden. People were trained to oversee emergency medical services, utilities, transportation, and other public works.

NOT-SO-FUN FACT	A worker at the Martin plant was discovered to be a follower of Adolph Hitler. Someone saw a "heil Hitler" sign in one of the new planes. ("Heil Hitler" was an expression showing support for Adolph Hitler, Germany's leader.) When investigating this, it was found that wires were cut and parts in the planes had been sabotaged (intentionally destroyed by an enemy). A man named Michael Etzel was arrested and sentenced to fifteen years in prison for those deeds.

Soon after war was declared, a system of spotter stations or listening posts was established by the U.S. military along the coastlines of the United States. People assigned to these stations watched for enemy planes. One of these spotter stations was one mile west of Frederick on a hill with a good view of the surrounding countryside and sky.

FUN FACT	Some Frederick County merchants donated their delivery wagons to the cause, to be ready for use as ambulances. They always had stretchers and pillows on board so they would be prepared if there was an emergency call.

Women in Frederick County took an active role on the home front. They volunteered in the American Women's Voluntary Services (a national organization) and the Volunteer Office and Citizen Service Corps. They recruited for the Wacs, Waves, and SPARS (women's divisions of the army, navy, and Coast Guard).

NOT-SO-FUN FACT	The most difficult job of the American Women's Voluntary Service was to deliver casualty telegrams to families of men who had been killed in the war.

Near Frederick, a prisoner-of-war camp was located that began operating in mid-1944. The camp held about two hundred prisoners, who worked for local farms and businesses. For exercise, the men played soccer on a field which they leveled themselves for that purpose.

Throughout World War II, the Selective Service was actively recruiting men to fight in the war. Many men enlisted. Others were drafted as the war dragged on.

During World War II, those northern Marylanders who were not fighting in the war were most likely involved in support activities at home. The first chapter of the American Women's Voluntary Services was organized in Bel Air in **Harford County.** The group started in 1941, manning the air raid system at the Bel Air Armory. Among other things, they also sold war bonds and prepared a manual on civil defense.

A group of volunteers called Gray Ladies helped in hospitals. These women wrote letters for patients wounded in the war; they also read to them and kept them company.

Because of the nearby location of the Aberdeen Proving Ground and Edgewood Arsenal, it was feared that Harford County would be attacked sometime during the war. Spotters watched the sky on three-hour shifts and called in any suspicious sightings. There may have been as many as forty observation posts in Harford County.

After the war began in Europe, the people in **Carroll County** began to plan for United States involvement. The American Red Cross, headquartered in Westminster, directed many of the county's prewar efforts. It prepared citizens with practice alerts and blackouts (every window covered so no light could be seen from outside).

During the war, industries grew quickly, taking the younger people away from farming. Farms did continue to prosper because crops were needed for U.S. soldiers and allies in Europe.

Other Wars

Northern Marylanders have served in other conflicts since World War II. People from these counties served their country in the Korean War, the Vietnam War, and the Persian Gulf War. Camp Detrick (later Fort Detrick), the Aberdeen Proving Ground, and Edgewood Arsenal were very active during these wars.

THE LATE TWENTIETH CENTURY

Lifestyles

The population in all four northern Maryland counties increased at a rapid rate toward the end of the twentieth century. A building boom occurred as farmland was developed to accommodate the growing population. New housing included condominiums and townhouses.

By the 1960s, developers began to construct shopping malls. These required many new employees. Large corporations moved to the area, bringing additional jobs and adding to the growth of the economy. The technology that created computers and microwaves made life easier.

In **Baltimore County,** horseback riding and breeding horses are activities enjoyed by many residents. Some families participate in fox hunts, cross-country racing, and jousting, the state sport.

As of 1995, there were 149 thoroughbred horse farms in Baltimore County. For a long time, the county has been considered the heart of Maryland's horse country. *FUN FACT*

Because of the large number of farms in **Frederick County,** people join such organizations as the Farm Bureau, the Grange, and the Breeder's Association. The Frederick Fair has been held once a year since the Civil War. In addition, many other festivals are held, like the Country Peddler Show, the Annual Frederick Art and Craft Fair, and the Maryland Christmas Fair. The Weinberg Center for the Arts offers silent films as well as plays, musicals, ballets, and concerts performed by national touring companies. It is located in a restored movie theater built in 1926. Music lovers can hear the Frederick Symphony Orchestra and the Frederick Youth Orchestra. The Delaplaine Center for the Visual Arts gives artists in the area a place to develop their talent and display their work.

The rapid rate of growth in **Harford County** contributed to a changing lifestyle during the last half of the twentieth century. Interstate 95 provides a fast way to reach cultural events in Baltimore City, Washington, D.C., and New York. The many bodies of water such as the Chesapeake Bay, the Susquehanna River, and Deer Creek provide opportunities for boating, fishing, and picnicking.

Agriculture was **Carroll County**'s primary industry for many years. As in Harford County, many new homes have been built in areas that were once farmland. Residents enjoy golfing, hiking, biking, and trout fishing at the Morgan Run Environment Area. Proximity (closeness) to ski areas in western Maryland provides another source of recreation.

Transportation

Many interstate highways make traveling easier in northern Maryland. Interstate 95 (also known as the John F. Kennedy Highway) runs through Harford and Baltimore counties.

The Baltimore Beltway (I-695) surrounds the city of Baltimore. I-895 connects the beltway and the city. Interstates 70 to Frederick County, 795 to Carroll County, 83 to Pennsylvania, and 95 to Harford and Cecil counties form spokes leading out from the Baltimore Beltway. In addition, there are three U.S. highways—Routes 1, 40, and 140—running through the northern Maryland region.

Several rail lines serve the northern Maryland area. In **Baltimore County,** they include CSX and Conrail, which carry freight. The

MARC (Maryland Rail Commuter) and Amtrak carry passengers. The light rail runs from Owings Mills and Timonium in Baltimore County into Baltimore City.

Frederick County's network of roads and highways includes Interstate 70, an east-west highway that runs in a northwesterly direction past Frederick. Interstate 270 runs north and south and connects with Interstate 495, which is the Washington Beltway in Montgomery County. A north-south road, U.S. 15, travels southwesterly past Frederick. U.S. 40 runs east and west through Frederick. U.S. 340 runs southwest across the Potomac to Harpers Ferry, West Virginia, and on into Virginia. The county has MARC train service and connection to Amtrak. MARC passengers stop at Point of Rocks Railroad Station, which dates back to the late 1800s.

Railroad service includes CSX and Maryland Midland. The Frederick Municipal Airport serves the county with small jet and turboprop charter service. County residents also use Baltimore-Washington Airport in Anne Arundel County and Dulles Airport in Virginia.

In **Harford County,** Amtrak, MARC trains, and a bus line provide service around the county and commuter service into Baltimore. Small plane owners (and those who rent planes) can go to one of Harford's three airports. The Harford County Airport is in Aldino. Fallston Airport and Forest Hill Industrial Airpark also serve county residents.

The Interstate 95 Millard E. Tydings Bridge over the Susquehanna River opened in 1963. President John F. Kennedy attended the dedication ceremony and cut the red ribbon, allowing cars to travel over the bridge for the first time.

FUN FACT

Carroll County residents and visitors have many choices of transportation. Route 140 runs through the county from east to west. Residents can ride the buses of the Carroll County Transit System. Charter bus companies also provide service in the county, as do forty-two motor freight (truck) lines. CSX Railroad and Maryland Midland Railway (short line) run through the county. The Carroll County Regional Airport/Jack B. Poage Field is close to Westminster. County residents also have close access to Baltimore-Washington International Airport, Dulles Airport, and Ronald Reagan Washington National Airport.

Courts and Public Service Agencies

Courts

The District Court of Maryland is headed by judges who are appointed by the governor with consent of the state senate. This court hears cases concerning landlord-tenant disagreements and motor vehicle violations. It hears criminal cases if the sentence would be less than three years in prison or the fine less than $2,500 (or both if they apply). It also hears civil cases involving penalties up to $20,000. The district court has no juries, so if a crime requires a jury, it must be tried in circuit court.

The District Court of Maryland for **Baltimore County** has thirteen judges appointed by the governor with consent of the senate. This is the only court in District 8. Court is held in Towson. Other district court buildings are located in Catonsville, Owings Mills, and Essex.

The District Court for **Frederick County** has three judges appointed by the governor with consent of the senate. District court is held in the courthouse at Courthouse Square, 100 W. Patrick Street, Frederick. District 11 includes Frederick and Washington counties.

The District Court of Maryland for **Harford County** (District 9) has four judges appointed by the governor with consent of the senate. District court is located in the Mary Risteau Building on Bond Street in Bel Air.

The District Court for **Carroll County** has two judges appointed by the governor with consent of the senate. They serve ten-year terms. District court is held in the Courthouse Annex on Court Place in Westminster. District 10 includes Carroll and Howard counties.

The circuit court of each county is part of a judicial circuit that usually includes other counties. Circuit court judges are appointed by the governor with approval from the state senate. Judges must also get voter approval every fifteen years for continued service, and they must retire when they are seventy years old. Circuit court hears criminal cases, serious civil cases, and juvenile cases. It hears cases regarding condemnation of land. This happens when the state wants to use a landowner's property for a highway, a state park, or a state building. The court also hears appeals from the district court.

Orphans court is also part of the circuit court, hearing cases concerning wills and estates. Its judges are elected by the voters of the county.

The Circuit Court of **Baltimore County** is part of the third judicial circuit, which includes Harford County. Its sixteen judges are appointed by the governor with approval from the senate. Circuit court is held in the county court building in Towson.

The Circuit Court of **Frederick County** is part of the sixth judicial circuit, which includes Montgomery County. There are four judges. Court is held in the Frederick County courthouse at 100 W. Patrick Street in Frederick.

The Circuit Court of **Harford County** has five judges. Circuit court is located in the courthouse in Bel Air. The circuit court is part of the third judicial circuit, which also includes Baltimore County.

The Circuit Court of **Carroll County** began as the Carroll County Court. The name was changed in 1851 to Circuit Court. Today, the court's three judges are appointed for fifteen-year terms. Court in the fifth judicial circuit is held in the historic courthouse in Westminster.

Also included in the judicial branch of each county government is the Registrar of Wills, who is an elected official.

Law Enforcement Agencies

Maryland state troopers have statewide authority. They patrol state roads and have agreements to work with other agencies if needed. They generally don't enter areas patrolled by other agencies unless invited or pursuing a criminal. They respond to calls concerning vandalism, robbery, drug use, domestic violence, assault, murder, and many other civil and criminal problems. Troopers also patrol the roads in the counties watching for drunk drivers, speeders, and reckless drivers. A number of the troopers have dogs who work with them. Some dogs are trained to sniff out drugs and to track people who are either lost or wanted by the police. Others are patrol dogs and attack dogs.

The Maryland state troopers in **Baltimore County** serve the county from their headquarters on Reisterstown Road in Pikesville and at Barrack "R" at Golden Ring.

Barrack "B" of the Maryland State Police in **Frederick County** is located on 1001 W. Patrick Street in Frederick. A weigh station and inspection facility is on Route 70 at New Market.

The troopers of the Maryland State Police serve **Harford County** from their barracks located in Benson on Route 1 near Bel Air.

FUN FACT   When the first state police barracks opened in 1939, there were no ambulances. When an accident was reported, the troopers responded in an old hearse or a bread truck. The injured person was put in the back and driven to the hospital. The sight of a hearse was probably not very encouraging to the accident victim!

The Maryland State Police have an office on Interstate 95. The officers assigned there work only on I-95, patrolling from the Delaware line to the tunnel throughway in Baltimore.

The Maryland State Police in **Carroll County** serve the county from their barracks at 1100 Baltimore Boulevard in Westminster.

Northern Maryland is also served by the state police MedEvac helicopter that is stationed at Frederick Airport. The MedEvac can be on the scene in a matter of minutes to fly critically ill or injured people to the hospital. It also helps local law enforcement agencies in rescues, and in finding people who are lost or trying to evade capture.

In each county, the office of sheriff represents the authority and interests of the state. The sheriff is in charge of detention of prisoners, security at courts, law enforcement, and serving of court papers such as subpoenas and arrest warrants. Before 1676, the sheriffs were appointed by the justices of the courts. The office of the sheriff has a long history dating back a thousand years. It began in England in 992 A.D. The officer was called a "shire-reeve." Eventually, this was shortened to sheriff.

In the colonies, the sheriff's duties included collecting taxes, taking a census (count) of people living in the county, reporting county happenings to the governor, and enforcing the law. The office of sheriff was originally a job that was appointed by the governor. After 1676, the court provided three names to the governor, who selected one of them to serve as sheriff for two years. After 1699, sheriffs served for three years. In 1776, the job was made an elected post.

The Office of the Sheriff in **Baltimore County** is located in the county court building on Bosley Avenue in Towson. About forty deputies assist the sheriff. Security system guards work at the courthouses.

The **Frederick County** Sheriff's Department has three bureaus: Administration, Operations, and Corrections. The sheriff's department offers several special outreach programs such as the Adopt-A-School Program and the Community Assistance Patrol (CAP), which promote safety and cooperation in the community. The department has offices in Brunswick, Emmitsburg, and Frederick. Two deputy sheriffs serve both Middletown and Myersville.

The towns of Frederick, Thurmont, Emmitsburg, Burkittsville, and Brunswick also have their own police departments.

The **Harford County** Sheriff's Office is in Bel Air. The department has its own training academy for deputies. Officers from other police agencies can also be trained there. The sheriff's office has a SWAT team. SWAT stands for special weapons and tactics. The team responds to hostage-taking and other dangerous situations needing their special skills.

The **Carroll County** Sheriff's Office is located at 100 N. Court Street in Westminster. The sheriff's office has a D.A.R.E. (Drug Abuse Resistance Education) program and a child support enforcement unit. Since there is no county police department, the sheriff's department handles traffic violations as well as crime.

Fire Departments

Fire was a constant hazard in early northern Maryland. Because there was no electricity, people used fire for heat, cooking, and light.

Fourteen companies formed the original **Baltimore County** Fire Department. Before 1881, volunteer fire departments were located in areas where many people lived. In 1881, six new fire trucks were ordered by the county commissioners to serve other parts of the county. The Baltimore County Fire Department was established by the state legislature and began operating in January 1882.

In April 1893, Towson established a fire company that had one hook and ladder wagon and one engine with chemicals to put out certain types of fires. The Towson Water Company laid pipes and put in fire hydrants to aid in fighting fires.

Baltimore County now has a Fire Rescue Academy in Towson where future firemen and paramedics are trained to handle fire situations. Training fires are set in a brick "smokehouse." There is a seventy-four foot tower and a chamber for gas-mask training, as well as oil pits, fire alarms, and other training items.

FUN FACT	The water pipes that carried water for fire fighting were made of wood.

In 1760, **Frederick County** organized its first fire department. A lottery was held to raise five hundred dollars for a new fire engine. By 1813, the department was called the Friendship Fire Company.

In the late 1700s, the city of Frederick required all homes to keep a leather bucket handy so people could supply water to fire engines in case of fire. Since there was no public water, all citizens helped put out fires. They formed water-bucket lines to pass water from the water source to the firefighters.

In 1817, the city of Frederick was divided into four fire wards (areas) and each ward had its own fire department. All white men who paid taxes were required to serve in the company in the ward where they lived.

NOT-SO-FUN FACT	In the mid-1800s, each fire company in Frederick also had a military company which was part of the Sixteenth Maryland Regiment. In 1859, there was a raid of the United States Armory at Harpers Ferry, West Virginia. It was led by John Brown, who had encouraged slaves to leave their masters and assist him in his efforts. Instead, they sided with their masters, believing that John Brown was a slave trader. The Frederick fire departments' military units were sent to assist in securing Harpers Ferry after Brown's attack. Brown and his men were later executed for their raid. This was one of the early skirmishes that led to the Civil War.	

One of Frederick's oldest fire engines, the "Lily of the Swamp," could pump water 274 feet. It was used for fifty-four years. It was donated to the Smithsonian Institution on February 23, 1933.

The firemen who operated the "Lily of the Swamp" were called the "Johnny Swampers."   *FUN FACT*

The National Fire Academy is located in Emmitsburg in Frederick County. It is a training center for firefighters and emergency personnel from around the country. Each year, the National Memorial Service for Fallen Firefighters is held there.

In **Harford County,** a lottery was held in 1834 to raise money to buy fire equipment, but it wasn't until 1890 that the first fire department was started. The Bel Air Volunteer Fire Department had its beginnings at a public meeting held in 1890. As a result, articles of incorporation were submitted to the county clerk for the Bel Air Fire and Salvage Company. The Aberdeen Fire Company was probably formed the same year. The Susquehanna Hose Company in Havre de Grace was formed in 1902. This company also responds to water rescues in the Susquehanna River. Today, each community in Harford County has a volunteer fire company. Harford County also has dedicated crews of ambulance personnel who respond to situations where people are ill or involved in accidents. These firefighters and ambulance personnel are not paid. All are volunteers!

In the early days of fire fighting, some towns required all men to attend fire drills. Taneytown in **Carroll County** enforced this regulation by charging twenty-five cents to all men between eighteen and fifty who did not attend.

The Carroll County Volunteer Firemen's Association was formed in 1923 to organize all the local companies in the various towns. There are now fourteen fire companies in Carroll County. The fire and ambulance services are coordinated by the Carroll County dispatch system. The fire marshall of Carroll County is appointed by the state fire marshall.

BALTIMORE COUNTY (1659)

Baltimore County is unique in that it surrounds Baltimore City on the north, east, and west. It has a combination of urban and rural life. Baltimore County is known for its horse farms. It is ranked third in the United States behind Lexington, Kentucky, and Ocala, Florida.

The Chesapeake Bay, the county's rivers, and its rolling countryside provide many scenic places to visit. The county has three main reservoirs—Loch Raven, Prettyboy, and Liberty—that supply water and recreation to county residents. Baltimore City also gets its water from Loch Raven and Liberty.

By the 1990 census, 692,134 people were living in Baltimore County. It is estimated that by the year 2010, there may be as many as 739,000.

Establishment of the County

Baltimore County is thought to have been established in 1659. It was the sixth Maryland county to be established. At that time, it was much larger than it is today. It included land in northeast and central Maryland on the western shore of the Bay, as well as some areas of the Eastern Shore. Today, that original larger area is often referred to as Old Baltimore County. Not much is known about Old Baltimore County's political history before January 12, 1659. On that day, an election was held so the citizens of the county could choose representatives (called burgesses) for the next session of the Maryland legislature. For this election to be held, the county's existence must have been recognized some time before January 12, 1659.

County Seat

Before the establishment of a county seat, people traveled to St. Mary's City, the state capital, to transact all their legal matters. When the population of an area grew big enough, the people were allowed to establish a county with its own courts. Baltimore County was established in 1659, though its county seat wasn't named until 1674.

Baltimore County has had several county seats over the years. It is thought that until 1674, the judges of Old Baltimore County held court in their homes. These men were not lawyers, but they did act as judges. They lived in the region that later became Harford and Cecil counties. The first county seat was the town of Old Baltimore, located on the Bush River in what is now Harford County. The only facts known about the courthouse of Old Baltimore are that it was constructed of logs and it had dormer windows. The next county seat was at the town of Gunpowder from 1691 to 1709.

In 1709, the court was moved to the town of Joppa on the Gunpowder River in what is now Harford County. Originally known by the land grant name of Taylor's Choice, Joppa was the most important town in Baltimore County for fifty years. Because of its excellent harbor, trade could be handled with countries of Europe and the West Indies. When court was in session, people came to Joppa from all around for the big day. Vendors sold all sorts of merchandise, race tracks were jammed with visitors, and the governor and other wealthy gentlemen were sure to be there.

The county seat remained at Joppa until 1768. That year, the county government was moved to Baltimore Town (now Baltimore City). Baltimore Town was the county seat until the county and the city were separated in 1851. At that time, Towsontown became the county seat, and Towson is still the county seat today.

The courthouse in Towson was designed in 1854 by Thomas and James Dixon and Thomas Balbirnie. The courthouse was built of local marble and limestone. It was completed in 1856 at a cost of thirty thousand dollars.

The current offices of the Baltimore County executive and the county council offices are located in the courthouse.

FUN FACT   The first indoor plumbing in the town of Towson was in the courthouse. The toilets were called "water closets." Water to flush the toilets came down from tanks on the roof whenever the chain on the water closet was pulled.

Growth in the Twentieth Century

Baltimore County continued to grow during the twentieth century. The lower part of the Loch Raven Dam had been completed in 1883. After many problems with acquiring the land, the upper dam was finished in 1914. A second level of the upper dam was built in 1921–1922.

The Baltimore Beltway was completed in 1962. This route circles Baltimore City and allows drivers to avoid traveling through the city. Trolleys were no longer used in Towson after 1963.

In the mid- to late-1900s, people looking for jobs or for a lower tax rate moved out of Baltimore City into the county. Many individual homes, row houses, and apartment complexes were built. New businesses and industries were established.

County Government

After the Civil War, the Democratic Party became a strong force in Baltimore County politics. Ever since, Democrats have won the majority of elections. Some politicians have abused their power and engaged in illegal activities. County executives Dale Anderson and Spiro T.

Agnew were involved in abuses in the 1960s and 1970s. Other state and county officials were also convicted of illegal activities in office.

Before 1958, Baltimore County was governed by county commissioners. As the county grew, the citizens voted to change the form of government. A "charter" government (according to the system approved by the voters) was established in 1958. In this form of government, a county executive and a seven-member council are elected. The executive offices of Baltimore County include the county executive, the administrative officer, and the chief of intergovernmental relations, labor relations, and communications. These offices are all located in the old courthouse building on Washington Avenue in Towson.

Major Towns

Towson was named after Ezekiel Towson, who owned an inn at the intersection of York Road, Dulaney Valley Road, and Joppa Road. This tavern was known for its food and good entertainment. It was torn down many years ago.

When York Turnpike (later called York Road) was planned, Ezekiel Towson arranged to have it routed so it would run right past the door of his tavern. This ensured that the tavern would continue to have a growing business.

FUN FACT

Catonsville was named after Richard Caton (1763–1845), who married Mary Carroll, the daughter of Charles Carroll of Carrollton. Mary Carroll's father gave the couple a large estate as a wedding gift. This area later became known as Catonsville.

Cockeysville was named after the Cockey family, probably Judge Joshua Frederick Cockey, because most historical records trace back to Judge Cockey. The site was originally a village and train station on the North Central Railroad. It is believed that in 1838, the family donated the railroad station to Baltimore County. The Cockey Homestead, erected in 1812, still stands along York Road.

Reisterstown was named for the German immigrant John Reister, who bought land and built an inn there about 1761. The inn was constructed on a road that was soon called Reister's Town Turnpike (now Reisterstown Road). The town grew along the turnpike.

Pikesville was named after Zebulon Pike, an American general and explorer who discovered Pike's Peak in Colorado in 1806. The town was started by Dr. James Smith, who bought land along Reisterstown Pike in 1814. The most prominent building at that time was the U.S. Arsenal, built in 1816. An arsenal is a building used to store weapons. In 1888, the weapons were removed, and the building became the Confederate Soldiers Home.

Although Pikesville today is a predominantly Jewish community, before World War II it was primarily gentile (non-Jewish). At that time, there was much prejudice against Jews. Many housing developments had "No Jews Allowed" signs posted at their entrances.

The area that is now **Lutherville** was once several sections of land owned by different people, including one portion called Regulation. In 1852, John G. Morris purchased part of Regulation and founded the town of Lutherville, named in honor of Martin Luther.

Parkville is a melting pot of cultural diversity. It has many lovely neighborhoods, and the people who live there feel a strong sense of community.

Timonium means "veil of tears." The town was named after the mansion belonging to Mrs. Archibald Buchanan.

Oella is a historic mill town. The name appears on the original land patent to the Union Manufacturing Company in 1811. In 1887, William J. Dickey purchased the company after flood damage and economic depression forced its sale at auction. He renamed the company Oella Mills. These textile mills continued to be very successful into the late 1900s until devastating floods from tropical storm Agnes destroyed them in June 1972.

Dundalk was named in 1888 for Henry McShane's birthplace in Ireland. McShane owned the Central Foundry. The town was developed by Bethlehem Steel, the U.S. government, and private builders.

Essex is an English name meaning "the east section." It was once part of a colonial estate, Paradise Farm. In 1909, the farm was sold off in lots by the Taylor Land Company, and the first home was built in what is now Essex.

Middle River was once the home of the Glenn L. Martin Company, which built airplanes. Until 1929, the area was mostly farmland and recreation sites.

Sparrows Point was granted to Thomas Sparrow and named after him in 1652. His son Solomon built a home in the area and named it Sparrow's Nest. The family owned the land until 1886, when 1,000 acres of the estate were sold to the Pennsylvania Steel Company. The company drained the marshes. Bethlehem Steel bought the plant in 1916. The steel-mill workers lived in the town, which is still called Sparrows Point.

Owings Mills derives its name from Samuel Owings, Jr., who built three successful mills—Upper Mill, Lower Mill, and Middle Mill—along Reisterstown Road. All the mills ground flour. These mills used "ULM" as their trademark. The site of these mills became known as Owings Mills and grew into a thriving community. Today it is the location of the studios for Maryland Public Television.

Churches and Religion

Early settlers of Baltimore County had to travel a great distance over poor roads to attend church. Only a few churches existed.

About 1691, the Church of England (Anglican) became the established church in the colony. In Baltimore County, several parishes for this church were organized. Garrison Forest is one example.

Shortly before the Revolutionary War, Methodist ministers began to travel around the county, holding services wherever they could. Many times the service would be in someone's home. The Methodist Church grew quickly because of these clergymen. One of them was Francis Asbury, who later became the first Bishop of the Methodist Church in America.

In 1704, anti-Catholic laws were passed in Maryland. Priests could celebrate mass only in a private home, and Catholic children were not allowed to attend school. A Catholic could not inherit anything from his family without giving up the faith. Most of the people living in Baltimore County in the mid-1700s were Protestant. Yet in Baltimore County, the courts were tolerant of Catholics. There was even a tolerance for the Quakers, whom many people disliked because their religion did not permit them to take an oath, serve in the military, or take their hats off in court.

By the 1800s, more people had settled in the county. Camp meetings stirred interest in religion, and churches began to spring up in communities all over the county.

During this century, many Jewish families moved from Baltimore City into the county, and Baltimore County now has a large Jewish population.

Education and Schools

Because the population of Baltimore County was so spread out in the early years, no schools were established in the county. Wealthy families hired tutors (home teachers) or sent their children away to school. But for most children, education was a form of apprenticeship. The child would be an apprentice (helper) to a tradesman, thus learning the trade. Eventually some schools opened, but many soon closed because students had to travel too far to reach them. Some business people banded together and started a school for their children. Churches began to school the children in the congregations to be sure they learned to read the Bible. Presbyterian and Jesuit congregations taught both boys and girls to read. Not all schools accepted girls. Some parents hired people to teach their children a skill such as sewing or an art such as music.

In the early 1900s, a child as young as fourteen could be the substitute teacher for an elementary school class if the teacher could not be there.   *FUN FACT*

Schools for black children were officially established in Baltimore County on February 20, 1872. At that time, the board of education gave fifty dollars to each "colored school" in the county that had at least twenty students. In 1872, the school board reported that the black schools were very similar to the white schools in salaries paid to the teachers and in the rules and regulations governing them. The same textbooks were used. The biggest problems for all schools were finding good teachers and finding buildings to house the schools. The first black high schools were built in 1939. They were Carver High School in Towson, Banneker High School in Catonsville, and Bragg High School in Sparrows Point. Although these high schools existed, many black students did not attend school at all after the seventh grade because it was too difficult for them to reach the schools.

John Wilkes Booth, the man who shot President Abraham Lincoln, went to schools in Bel Air, Catonsville, and Baltimore City in Maryland, as well as in York, Pennsylvania.   *FUN FACT*

The oldest public high school in Baltimore County is Franklin High School, which was established in 1820 as the Franklin Academy.

As of 1997, 165 private schools were in the county. One of the oldest is the Hannah More Center School, originally called the Hannah More Academy, founded in 1832. It was established as an Episcopal boarding school and is the oldest of these in the United States.

Baltimore County also has some fine colleges and universities: Towson University; University of Maryland, Baltimore County, in Catonsville; Goucher College; and Villa Julie College. Three community colleges are in the county: Catonsville, Dundalk, and Essex.

Businesses, Industries, and Agriculture

The earliest businesses in Baltimore County were farms. Tobacco was an important crop because it was used as money. Soil in the area was not the best for growing tobacco. In the early 1800s, people began to prosper due to the growth of Baltimore City as a grain port. Wheat became the most popular crop. Livestock was also raised. Many farms were dairy farms, such as the Wilton Farm Dairy which was in business almost one hundred years. Farming was the most important business until the mid-1900s.

Today, beef cattle and poultry are raised, and grains and hay are grown. There are fewer dairy farms because of health and sanitation laws that make dairy farming more expensive and difficult. Horse farms such as Sagamore Farm are well known.

Baltimore County has many streams, and its location on the fall line was perfect for building mills. In the 1600s and 1700s, gristmills and sawmills opened; there were also paper mills, forges, and iron furnaces.

NOT-SO-FUN FACT	Since Maryland had no child labor laws until 1873, children as well as adults worked long hours in the mills for very little pay.

The first paper mill in Maryland was located on the Gunpowder Falls in the northern part of the county. It was owned by William Hoffman, a German immigrant.

FUN FACT	The Hoffman mill supplied paper to the Continental Congress.

Ships traveled up and down the Chesapeake Bay, selling pig iron made in the furnaces. Iron was also sold to England.

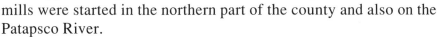

When the railroads were built in the 1800s, farmers and businessmen began shipping their products by rail to more distant markets. Mills and factories started the Industrial Revolution in Maryland. The railroads provided a way to market goods, so businesses began to enlarge and modernize. Cotton factories became a big industry along the Patapsco River, the Gunpowder River, Jones Falls, and Gwynn's Falls. Iron furnaces and copper-rolling mills were established. Paper mills were started in the northern part of the county and also on the Patapsco River.

Numerous small family-owned businesses sprang up during the 1800s and early 1900s. Many of them closed in the mid-1900s, when huge grocery stores and large malls took business away. The first major department store chain to move to the suburbs was Hutzler's.

Once Baltimore County's largest employer, Bethlehem Steel at Sparrows Point has had many ups and downs in its history. The company was built on farmland bought in 1887. Later, more land was bought to enlarge the plant. The company also built a town for its employees and schools for their children. Workers had health care and other benefits. The company would import ore from Cuba, and produce steel products. One of its most important products was railroad tracks. While the company enjoyed much success, it did have problems such as accidents involving workers, a strike in 1959, and clashes with law enforcement agencies and environmental groups over pollution of the Chesapeake Bay. The work force changed from thirty thousand people before 1959 to less than ten thousand during the 1980s. Today, Bethlehem Steel is once again Baltimore County's largest employer. Other large employers are AAI Corporation, Sweetheart Cup, Black and Decker, Lockheed Martin Aero and Naval Systems, Baltimore Gas and Electric, Bell Atlantic of Maryland, Blue Cross–Blue Shield of Maryland, Greater Baltimore Medical Center, the U.S. Social Security

Administration, McCormick and Company, Proctor and Gamble, St. Joseph's Hospital, and Baltimore County Public Schools.

FUN FACT	Headquarters for eight Fortune 500 companies are located in Baltimore County. The county has the largest number of research scientists in the United States.

Jobs that will be important in the future of Baltimore County are those involving research and development or tourism. Research and development companies invent things to make life easier. Many tourists are coming to Baltimore County. Better transportation and more hotels, restaurants, and gift shops will be needed.

Fascinating Folks (Past and Present)

Benjamin Banneker was a famous black scientist, mathematician, and writer. He was born in a one-room log cabin on his father's farm near what is now Catonsville. His father was a blacksmith and a tobacco farmer. Benjamin was very smart and had many interests, but his favorite subjects were science and math. When he was twenty-two, he built an amazing wooden clock that worked perfectly. He was befriended by the Ellicott brothers of Ellicott's Mills across the Patapsco River. When Major Andrew Ellicott was asked to survey an area of land for the nation's capital, Benjamin was asked to work on the project too. Benjamin also published an almanac every year for seven years. Each year, he sent a copy of the almanac to Thomas Jefferson to show that black people were capable of doing the same things that white people did.

NOT-SO-FUN FACT	During Benjamin Banneker's funeral in 1806, his house burned down and with it went many things that would have been valuable artifacts today, including the wooden clock and all his books and papers.

Major General Nathan Towson was a captain in the War of 1812. After the war, he was promoted to lieutenant colonel and served as paymaster general of the U.S. Army. He served in the Mexican War and became a major general in 1849. He was related to Ezekiel Towson, after whom the county seat is named.

Charles Ridgely once owned a 1,500-acre estate north of Towson. Today, Goucher College is on part of that estate. The Ridgely family owned an iron furnace. This furnace is now covered by the Loch Raven Reservoir. Charles Ridgely's son, **Captain Charles Ridgely,** and his wife **Rebecca** built the Hampton Mansion, which has thirty-five rooms. Very few towns existed in the time of Charles and Rebecca Ridgely, so large manors became the centers where people met socially. Hampton was one of these manors, and today, it is open for tours.

After their house was finished, the Ridgelys had a housewarming. Charles Ridgely liked to enjoy parties, but his wife was very religious and preferred singing religious songs. So the housewarming was held in two parts. Rebecca Ridgely and her friends celebrated at one end of the house singing and praying, and her husband and his friends celebrated at the other end drinking and partying.

Unfortunately, Charles died six months after the house was built.

FUN FACT

William Hoffman was the first papermaker in Maryland. His first mill was built on the Gunpowder Falls in 1775. He made paper used for writing and wrapping.

Rosa Ponselle was a famous opera singer who made her home in Baltimore County after her retirement. She assisted many young singers with their careers and helped to establish the Baltimore Opera Company.

Donald and Mary Grempler started a real estate business that has grown to be one of the largest in the United States. The business was opened in 1960 by Mary Grempler.

In 1963, her husband joined the business. Theirs was one of the first real estate companies to use computers and to develop a real estate software program for the company's own use.

Although it was her business, Mary Grempler gave it her husband's name (Donald E. Grempler Realty) because she was afraid no one would come to a real estate company run by a woman.

FUN FACT

Nancy Claster, born in 1915 in Baltimore, married a television producer and worked as a nursery school teacher. When her husband produced an educational television show for children, she became the television teacher. The show was called *Romper Room,* and the children called her Miss Nancy. The show aired on WBAL-TV. It was so popular that the CBS network aired it all over the United States and in forty-five other countries around the world. Nancy Claster died April 25, 1997, at the age of eighty-two.

Nan Hayden Agle grew up in Catonsville. She wrote many books for children, including *The Three Boys* series, *Princess Mary of Maryland*, and *My Animals and Me*.

Roger Caras is one of America's leading animal-rights activists. He is a past president of the American Society for the Prevention of Cruelty to Animals in New York. He was a special reporter on animals and the environment for the ABC network and won an Emmy Award for his work. Mr. Caras wrote a book about animals. He lives in Freeland.

The Loizeaux family of Towson owns the world-famous demolition company, Controlled Demolition, Inc. Employees who are experts in their field "implode" buildings precisely (they fall inward and do not damage neighboring buildings). The company was started by **Jack Loizeaux** in 1947. It has demolished over seven thousand buildings all over the world, including the thirty-three story J. L. Hudson Department Store in Detroit and the ruins left after the terrorist bombing of the Murrah Federal Building in Oklahoma City. Movies such as *Lethal Weapon 3*, *Demolition Man*, and *Enemy of the State* show implosions staged by Controlled Demolition, Inc.

Richard L. Waldrep is one of Baltimore County's best-known artists. He designed a set of stamps for the U.S. Postal Service, commemorating the 1996 Summer Olympics in Atlanta. He also designed six stamps for the 1992 Summer Olympic Games in Barcelona, Spain.

John Unitas and **Artie Donovan** played for the Baltimore Colts and are still two of Maryland's most famous sports heroes. They played in the 1958 championship game often called the greatest football game ever played.

Pam Shriver, a professional tennis player since 1979, is one of the top players in the world. She is also a part-owner of the Baltimore Orioles baseball team. She organizes many charity events.

Cal Ripken, Jr., and his family now live in Baltimore County. He is described in greater detail in the Harford County chapter.

Many television personalities live in Baltimore County. **Stan Stoval** (news anchor), **Jamie Costello** (news anchor), **Veronica Johnson** (weather anchor), and **Keith Cate** (news anchor) all work for WMAR-TV, channel 2. **Marty Bass** (morning anchor and weather), **Don Scott** (morning anchor), **John Buren** (sports anchor), **Bob Turk** (weather anchor), and **Sally Thorner** (news anchor) are on WJZ-TV, channel 13. **Marianne Banister** (news anchor and reporter), **Tim Tooten** (education reporter), and **Gerry Sandusky** (sportscaster) are on WBAL-TV, channel 11. **Denise Saunders** (news anchor) and **Bruce Cunningham** (sports) live in the county also.

Jim McKay was an ABC sports anchor. For many years he hosted ABC's *Wide World of Sports*. He is very involved in the horse racing industry. He was instrumental in starting the Maryland Million Horse Race run every October at Laurel Race Track. He lives in Monkton.

In addition, well-known sports figures and celebrities too numerous to list live in Baltimore County.

Natural Resources

Many streams flow through Baltimore County, helping farmers and providing fishing fun.

In the past, marble was an important natural resource in Baltimore County. Marble was mined at a quarry near what is now Cockeysville. The marble was considered to be very high quality.

Some very important buildings were built with marble mined at the Cockeysville quarry. Some of them are the Washington Monument in Baltimore, part of the Washington Monument in Washington, D.C., Eutaw Place Baptist Church in Baltimore, the Peabody Conservatory in Washington, and the steeples of the famous St. Patrick's Cathedral in New York City. The quarry is now under the waters of the Beaver Dam.

FUN FACT

Limestone was also mined in the county starting about 1804. Most of it was used in the farming and building industries. These quarries are now filled with water. Iron was another natural resource that was mined in the county.

Soils in the county include clay (used for making bricks), loam, and sand.

The Patapsco, Gunpowder, Middle, and Back rivers were important in the past as a source of power for the mills that were built along their shores. Today they provide sites for parks and places of recreation.

Fish such as the popular rockfish are a natural resource of the county, as are blue crabs, oysters, and clams. People can enjoy the water at the county's numerous beaches.

Places of Interest

The **Milton Inn** on York Road in Sparks is a fieldstone house that was built from 1818 to 1823. It originally served as a stagecoach stop. Later it became a boys academy. One of its students was John Wilkes Booth from Harford County. The inn later became a restaurant.

The **Fire Museum of Maryland,** opened in 1971, is located in Lutherville. Over fifty pieces of antique fire equipment show how fire fighting changed from 1822 to 1957. Some of this equipment was used to fight the Great Fire of Baltimore in 1904. The museum also has a badge and uniform collection, fire alarms, and videos of fires that occurred in the area. Books and other items are available at the gift shop.

The **Hampton Mansion** is so big it took seven years to build. It was finished in 1790 and is the largest example of eighteenth-century Georgian-style architecture in America that is still standing. Located in Towson, it was built by Captain Charles Ridgely, who made a fortune in the ironworks business. This mansion shows how a wealthy family lived in the late 1700s. There are formal gardens to enjoy. At one time, the gardens at Hampton were watered by a system made up of 10,590 feet of wooden pipes that brought water from nearby springs. Many trees on the property have died. The remaining trees are over 130 years old.

Inside, in the dining room, there is a flytrap. This is a glass plate filled with sugar and water, and covered with a glass dome with a hole in the top. The flies would enter and could not get out. Another interesting item is a swooning couch. At that time, it was fashionable for a woman to have a small waist. Women would wear very tight corsets (undergarments), which often caused them to faint (swoon). The swooning couch provided a place to fall.

In the winter of 1842, one of the children who lived in the Hampton Mansion wrote an account of a snowball fight that started outside and moved inside the big house. Snowballs flew around the beautifully decorated Great Hall, which is about the size of a basketball court. That same winter, boys threw snowballs at the girls in one of the bedrooms.

Seven generations of the Ridgely family lived at Hampton from 1788 to 1948. One of Maryland's governors, Charles Carnan Ridgely, also lived there. The Hampton National Historic Site is now owned and operated by the National Park Service.

Many other historic homes and grounds with interesting names are located in the southern part of the county. Some of them include Prospect Hill, Venture, Henry's Delight, Littlecote, Summerfield, and Blythyn-a-Cambria, which is a Welsh name.

The **Thomas Viaduct** at Relay is believed to be one of the oldest stone arched railroad bridges in the world. It is 60 feet high and 612 feet long and was named after Philip Thomas, the first president of the B&O Railroad.

Jericho Covered Bridge on Jericho Road in the Kingsville area links Harford and Baltimore counties across Little Gunpowder Falls. The 130-year-old white oak beams supporting the roof show no signs of decay.

Boordy Vineyard on Long Green Pike in Hydes was once a farm owned by Thomas Gittings. Surveyed for him in 1721, it was originally called "Gittings Choice." Tobacco was grown there before the Revolutionary War. After the war, wheat was the main crop. Now it is Maryland's oldest and largest winery. The winery was founded by Philip Wagner and is now owned by the DeFord family.

Gunpowder Copper Works was located near the bridge over Big Gunpowder Falls. It was owned by Levi Hollingsworth. Blocks of copper were shipped from England and rolled and shaped into items that could be sold. The copper used on the roof of the original Capitol building was rolled and prepared here. Visitors who ride through the area can see some of the buildings that were part of the copper works.

The **Baltimore County Historical Society** headquarters is located in Cockeysville in what was the county's last almshouse. Almshouses were shelters for the very poor and homeless. The historical society houses a large collection of artifacts from early Baltimore County life. In addition, a barn museum displays farm machinery and tools.

Ballestone Manor in Essex shows how prosperous farmers lived in the 1800s. Each year in September, a reenactment of a Civil War battle is held on the grounds.

The **Oella Historic District** was the site of the largest cotton mill in America in the early 1800s. It was named after the first woman cotton-spinner. The Union Manufacturing Company built the mill, and it was the first textile company chartered (licensed) by the state of Maryland. Over the years many explosions, fires, and floods caused much damage, and many buildings had to be replaced. The current building was built in 1918. The mill was closed in 1972, and the building now houses antique and specialty shops. On Oella Avenue is the **Oella–Benjamin Banneker Historical Park and Museum.**

Honoring famous African-Americans is the **Benjamin Banneker Memorial Obelisk,** on the grounds of Mt. Gilboa AME church in Oella.

Sagamore Farm in Glyndon is a horse farm given to Gwynne Vanderbilt as a birthday present when he was twenty-one. Many famous horses lived on this farm such as Native Dancer, Restless Dancer, and Globemaster.

When Maryland's only public television broadcasting station opened in Owings Mills on September 28, 1969, it was known as the Maryland Center for Public Broadcasting. Today, it is **Maryland Public Television (MPT).** Its broadcast area covers all of Maryland, parts of West Virginia, Virginia, Pennsylvania, and Delaware. Six transmitters are located in Annapolis, Salisbury, Hagerstown, Oakland, Frederick, and Baltimore.

Martin State Airport is located near the city of Middle River. Aviation was a growing business in the early 1900s. By 1930, several airplane factories and airports were located in the county. Glenn L. Martin, an airplane manufacturer from Kansas, bought the 1,200-acre Milburn farm in Middle River in 1929 and started building airplanes there. The planes were seaplanes that were capable of landing on land or water. The most famous of these was called the China Clipper.

The **Glenn L. Martin Aviation Museum** on Wilson Point Road in Middle River features the history of Maryland aviation. It shows airplanes from the 1920s to the present. The museum also has other items on display relating to the Glenn L. Martin Company.

Prettyboy Dam is located in the northern part of Baltimore County. A myth suggests the name is from a local farmer's love for his colt Prettyboy. The story claims this horse wandered into a nearby stream, slipped, sank in the marsh, and was never seen again. Actually, the name is from an old land grant. When the dam was built, the authorities named it Prettyboy Dam.

Baltimore County has several wineries. **Basignani Winery** on Falls Road in Sparks, **Woodhall Vineyards and Wine Cellars** in Parkton, and **Boordy Vineyards** in Hydes all have tours.

The **Maryland State Police Museum** is located on the grounds of the Maryland State Police headquarters on Reisterstown Road in Pikesville. Visitors can see pictures, artifacts, and equipment used by the state police throughout its history.

The **Maryland State Fair** is one of the biggest annual events in the state. Held at the Timonium Fairgrounds, it draws thousands of people every year. In 1878, Baltimore County Grange held a small, one-day agricultural fair. It was so successful that they decided to hold one every year. The Agricultural Society of Baltimore County was established to organize it. The first Timonium Fair was held in 1879, though was not considered a state fair at the time. It became so successful that in 1937, the Maryland General Assembly designated the fair at Timonium to be the official Maryland State Fair. Over the years, a racetrack was constructed with stables and exhibition halls. A railroad line brought people from Baltimore City to attend the fair.

Today the Maryland State Fair draws people from all over the state of Maryland and from southern Pennsylvania. It has carnival rides, concerts, craft exhibits, and many other attractions. The competition for the best farm animals and other farm products is a major event, and farm families work all year to try to win.

The **Maryland Hunt Cup** is another event that draws thousands of spectators every year. It is considered one of the two major steeplechase races in the world. (A steeplechase is a race in which the horses jump obstacles along a course.) The Maryland Hunt Cup is one of the oldest and most difficult horse races in the United States. It began on May 26, 1894, when two clubs, the Elkridge Hunt Club and the Green Spring Valley Hunt Club, held a cross-county steeplechase race. The course was four miles long. No jumps were built for the race; all the jumps were over logs or other naturally occurring obstacles.

After being held in various locations over the years, the race is held every year now in Glyndon in Worthington Valley.

Parks and Recreational Areas

In early Baltimore County, some types of recreation and sports were different than they are today. Fox hunting and horse racing were very popular sports in the late 1700s. When courts were in session, races were held in the county seats. Hunting for deer, wildcats, foxes, pheasants, grouse, and quail was also very popular.

The **Loch Raven Dam and Reservoir** are located on Dulaney Valley Road north of Baltimore City. They are part of a 2,400-acre park with boat rentals, a picnic area, and hiking trails. Visitors can also fish for large- and small-mouth bass, chain pickerel, crappies, and other fish. In 1922, the town of Warren and the Merryman's Mill were both flooded to enlarge the reservoir. Loch Raven is named for Luke Raven, a man who came from England and bought land in the county. At his death, he left the area of Loch Raven to his son Abraham.

Oregon Ridge Park and Nature Center is a 1,034-acre park in Cockeysville with a wide variety of activities—trails for downhill or cross-country skiing in the winter, a launching site for hang-gliding, nature trails, a greenhouse growing local plants, a forest ecosystem exhibit, and an archaeological dig.

Artifacts discovered at the archaeological dig at Oregon Ridge were found by Baltimore County schoolchildren who were allowed to dig there. A dwelling has been built on the original foundation of an 1850s storage shed.   *FUN FACT*

Gunpowder Falls State Park is made up of several sections located over a wide area of Baltimore and Harford counties along Gunpowder River Valley. It has a total of 17,000 acres. The main section of the park is located in the Hereford area along the Gunpowder River. In this section, there are 13,020 acres with over 100 miles of trails for hiking, biking, or riding horses. Twenty-one miles of the Northern Central Railroad Trail run through the park. There is a playground, and access to boating, fishing, and swimming.

Northern Central Railroad Trail starts north of Cockeysville in the town of Ashland and ends in Pennsylvania. The trail follows the old roadbed of the abandoned Northern Central Railroad. People can hike, jog, ride a bicycle, or go horseback riding along the portion of this scenic trail that is located within Gunpowder Falls State Park.

Hart-Miller Island State Park is an island located in the Chesapeake Bay near the mouth of Middle River. Reached only by boat, it offers 3,000 feet of beach and areas for picnicking and camping. Originally, two islands were on the site. When Baltimore's harbor was dredged, sand was dumped between the two islands, connecting them into one island.

Near Catonsville, **"# 9 Trolley Line"** is a hiking and biking trail. It follows the old trolley tracks from the end of Edmonson Avenue in Baltimore County to Ellicott City in Howard County.

Soldiers Delight Natural Environment Area is located on Deer Park Road in Owings Mills. It is owned by the Nature Conservancy, a national organization that buys land to save it from development. Visitors can hike and birdwatch along the nature trails.

Wild Acres Trail in Owings Mills is a habitat trail that was opened in 1989. It is about a mile long. The trail gives ideas about how to encourage birds, butterflies, and other wildlife to come into backyards.

Baltimore County has a number of public beaches, including **Miami Beach Park,** located near the place where Middle River empties into the Bay; **Oregon Ridge Beach and Park** in Cockeysville; and **Rocky Point Beach and Park** on Back River. Rocky Point is Baltimore County's largest waterfront park with over 700 feet of shoreline.

FREDERICK COUNTY (1748)

Frederick County can be considered the gateway to western Maryland because of the difference in topography (surface features) that occurs as the land changes from the Piedmont region to the Appalachian Mountain region. The Catoctin Mountains of Frederick County provide beautiful scenery for travelers on their way westward. In addition, a large number of historic buildings reflect the county's rich background.

In January 1997, the population of Frederick County was 183,045. By the year 2020, it is projected to reach 267,100.

Establishment of the County

In 1748, Frederick County split from Prince George's County, which at the time covered a large portion of western and central Maryland. Frederick was the fourteenth county established in Maryland, and it grew so fast that it became necessary to divide it into other counties. The sections south and west of South Mountain became four other counties: Washington and Montgomery counties in 1776, Allegany in 1789, and Garrett in 1872. In addition, Carroll County was formed out of western Baltimore County and the eastern part of old Frederick County in 1837. Frederick County celebrated its 250th anniversary in 1998.

It is not known how Frederick County was named, though there are two leading theories. Frederick County may have been named for Frederick Calvert, the sixth Lord Baltimore. However, it is also possible that it was named after the Prince of Wales, Frederick Lewis, who was the son of George II.

County Seat

Fredericktown was established by an Englishman, Daniel Dulany. He came to America in 1703 as an indentured servant and settled in Port Tobacco in Charles County. He worked in the law office of George Plater, who had paid for his passage to America. Dulany eventually became a lawyer, then a judge, a member of the Maryland General Assembly, and attorney general of Maryland. He began buying land in northern and western Maryland in the 1720s. Dulany and his friend Benjamin Tasker developed parcels of land in the area that became Frederick County. In 1745, Dulany laid out streets in what would become Fredericktown on the eastern edge of the tract of land known as Tasker's Chance. When Frederick County was formed in 1748, Fredericktown became the county seat. By 1750, Fredericktown had about two hundred homes. Though some colonists were English, most were German.

FUN FACT   A two-story brick tavern at the southwest corner of the town square in Fredericktown also served as the courthouse until the first courthouse was constructed in 1750 on Council Street.

The first jail was built in 1775. It was a two-story log building with a small house next door for the jailkeeper and guard.

Fredericktown's name was officially changed to Frederick when it was incorporated as a city in 1817.

Growth in the Twentieth Century

In Frederick County, the major change during the last century has been the shift from agriculture to business and industry. Although there is still much undeveloped land in the county, fewer than 8 percent of its people are now farmers. Many people who live in Frederick County work in Howard County, Baltimore, or Washington, D.C. People from Frederick County are proud of their ethnic diversity, which continues to expand.

During the early 1970s, construction in the county grew much too quickly for many residents. The county grew 34 percent in just ten years. People thought the commissioners were allowing growth to increase too fast without any plan. In 1978, they elected a totally new board of county commissioners.

The first bus company to provide service to Frederick was the Blue Ridge Lines. It was started in the 1920s by W. C. Hann, and was bought by Potomac Edison in 1938 and by Greyhound in 1955.

The improvement of Route 15 in the 1950s brought people and businesses to Frederick. The Frederick Shopping Center was opened in 1957. The opening of two malls in the 1970s caused problems for downtown businesses, because people no longer came into town to shop. In 1976, a flood damaged a large part of downtown, but residents and business owners did not give up. In the 1980s, they began the Carroll Creek Flood Control Project to try to prevent another flood. The result is a controlled creek (two culverts beneath the surface carry excess water to prevent floods). There is beautiful parkland and a pathway beside the creek. Businesses, restaurants, and theaters have moved back into town and are doing well.

Today growth is expected to continue because of the county's close location to Washington, D.C., and Montgomery County, where many government agencies are located. Many who work in those locations prefer to live in a more rural setting. Frederick County provides that.

County Government

In 1748, an act was passed by the General Assembly creating the Frederick County government.

Five county commissioners are elected at large for four-year terms. (This means anyone in the county can vote for them.) The commissioners see that state laws are carried out, and they pass laws for the county. They sit on various boards such as the public library, the board of education, social services, and economic and community development. The county attorney and treasurer are appointed by the county executive. The sheriff is elected.

Major Towns

The city of **Frederick** was originally called Fredericktown. It was founded in 1745 along trails used by Native Americans and early settlers. Many immigrants came from Germany and England. Frederick has two sister cities: Schifferstadt, Germany, and Morzheim, Germany. There is a sign noting Schifferstadt's special friendship at the entrance to Frederick, and a street is named for that town.

Emmitsburg was named after Samuel Emmit, who owned a large amount of land in the area in the 1700s. The town was settled along an old Indian trail that ran through York and Adams counties in Pennsylvania and traveled south into Maryland. The earliest German settlers in the area may have entered Maryland via this trail as early as 1710. The town was originally called Poplar Fields, then Silver Fancy, but was renamed after Emmit in 1786. Emmitsburg was incorporated in 1825 by the General Assembly. The Western Maryland Railroad arrived in 1875. Mt. St. Mary's College and St. Joseph's Female Academy are located there.

Thurmont was settled by Jacob Weller and his family. They came from Germany in the 1740s and bought land around 1751 near what is now Thurmont. In 1804, lots were surveyed and sold and other people settled there. The small community became known as Mechanicstown because of its craftsmen—wagonmakers, blacksmiths, tanners, and barrelmakers. The Western Maryland Railroad was built through the town in 1871. The railroad asked the town to change its name because there was a Mechanicsburg and a Mechanicsville on the line in Pennsylvania. The townspeople first selected Blue Mountain City, but that was too long a name for the post office. The name of the town was changed in 1894 to Thurmont.

Burkittsville is a small historic town which has remained virtually the same since it was founded in 1829. The post office there was called Harley's Store until the town was officially established. It was named after one of its settlers, Henry Burkitt. The town is near the location of the only monument to war correspondents in the United States. The hit movie *The Blair Witch Project* was filmed there in the late 1990s.

Knoxville began as a Native American trading post as early as 1728. It became known later for its distilleries (factories which made liquor). The Needwood and the Ahalt Distilleries produced liquor until the Eighteenth Amendment to the Constitution made it illegal to make or drink liquor. (This was known as Prohibition.) Most of the liquor was shipped by rail to markets in the cities. However, some of it was undoubtedly consumed in Knoxville's seven saloons.

Bartonsville is a town near New Market that was founded by a former slave, Greensberry Barton.

Middletown was settled by families of German Reformed and Lutherans who migrated from Pennsylvania, traveling down an old Indian trail to the Potomac River. This trail crossed the Middletown Valley and eventually became known as the Susquehanna and Potomac Road. Middletown was originally called Smithfield. The name was changed to Middletown in 1767 when George Michael Jesserang purchased the land and established the lots. Supposedly the name Middletown is based on the town's location midway between two mountains. Middletown was incorporated March 4, 1834.

Sabillasville was settled by Peter Zollinger, who originally named it Zollinger's Town. After his wife, Savilla, died, the town was renamed after her—Savillasville. The spelling changed over the years to Sabillasville.

Jefferson is an old town dating from 1779 that at one time was known as "The Trap" because a band of highway robbers had their headquarters there. The name was changed in 1832 to honor Thomas Jefferson.

New Market is located eight miles from Frederick. It was founded in 1793 by Nicholas Hall. Lord Baltimore had granted land there to John Dorsey, Jr., in 1743. Some early families to settle there were the Dorseys, the Hammonds, the Plummers, and the Burkitts.

Some unusual names of towns in Frederick County include Ijamsville, Ladiesburg, Lime Kiln, Wolfsville, Foxville, Hawbottom, and Shookstown.

Churches and Religion

Frederick County has many historic churches. In the city of Frederick, four of these churches are easy to find because of the spires (steeples) that are clearly visible anywhere in town. These are All Saints Episcopal Church (mid-1750s), Evangelical Lutheran Church with two spires (1855), Trinity Chapel (1763), and St. John the Evangelist Roman Catholic Church. This church was built some time after 1776 (when the law that forbade the building of Catholic churches was repealed). Before that time, Catholics worshiped in a home. Jewish worshipers have lived in the county since the mid-1700s. The first synagogue in Frederick County was built in 1919 in the town of Brunswick. The first German church in Maryland was built between 1732 and 1734 near Monocacy.

The land for St. Joseph's Chapel on Carrollton Manor in Buckeystown (1764) was donated by Charles Carroll of Carrollton, the only Catholic signer of the Declaration of Independence. Other historic churches are Middletown's Christ Reformed Church (built in 1818), Frederick Presbyterian Church (1825), Apple's Church in Thurmont (1826), Mount Carmel United Methodist Church on Baltimore Road at Sycamore Flats (1854), the Evangelical Reformed Church in Frederick (1848), and Eylers Valley Chapel in Sabillasville (1857).

Other congregations include African Methodist Episcopal, Baptist, Brethren, Christian and Missionary Alliance, Church of Jesus Christ of Latter-Day Saints, Lutheran, Moravian, Seventh-Day Adventist, United Church of Christ (formerly German Reformed), United Methodist, and many others.

Education and Schools

Over thirty-five thousand students study in Frederick County's elementary, middle, and high schools. The Rock Creek School and Diagnostic Center serves students with serious disabilities. The Heather Ridge School serves children with behavioral problems.

A number of fine private and parochial (operated by a religious group) schools are also located in the county. Some examples are Visitation Academy, St. John's Regional Catholic School, St. John's Literary Institute, Mother Seton School, Banner School, Frederick Christian Academy, New Life Christian School, the Seventh-Day Adventist School, and the Walkersville Christian Family Schools.

The Maryland School for the Deaf was established in 1867. It was built on the grounds of the Hessian Barracks, and it opened with thirty-four students.

Bentz Street Elementary School was the first to educate black children after the Civil War. The first black high school in Frederick was built in 1921 on West All Saints Street. Lincoln High School was the only secondary school for black students until 1962. Before it opened, black children could go to school only through the seventh grade. A marker now stands at the site of the school.

High school sports were segregated (black students played on separate teams). Lincoln teams played black high school teams from Hagerstown, Leesburg, and Cumberland.

When schools were segregated, education funds were not given equally to all schools, and this angered many black parents.

Hood College (founded in 1893) is a private coeducational four-year college. Another college in the county, Mt. Saint Mary's in Emmitsburg (founded in 1808), is a private four-year school. Frederick Community College offers an A.A. (Associate of Arts) degree in business and pre-engineering.

Businesses, Industries, and Agriculture

Early industries in Frederick County were based on the discovery of limestone, copper, slate, and flintstone that was used for making glass. Two glassmaking factories were located near Fredericktown, which created business with large cities such as New York and Philadelphia. Iron furnaces were built to manufacture pig iron, bar iron, and tools.

Today, well over four thousand businesses employ more than fifty-three thousand workers. Frederick County's largest employers are the National Cancer Institute at Fort Detrick, the Frederick County Board of Education, Frederick County Government, State Farm Insurance, Frederick Memorial Hospital, Prudential Home Mortgage, and Eastalco Aluminum. Additional large employers are Bio Whittaker, First Nationwide Mortgage, and Rotorex. Many antique shops are in the county, most of them located in Frederick and New Market.

In colonial times, the rich soil attracted many settlers. They could grow crops for their own use, and they could trade farm products for other necessities. Even today, the county is recognized for its rich soil.

FUN FACT	In 1790, more wheat was grown in Frederick County than in any other county in the United States. Although Frederick County is still considered mainly an agricultural county, the number of businesses and industries is growing.

Dairy farming is a major agricultural industry in Frederick County. It provides one-third of Maryland's milk production. Vegetable farming is also important. Over 200,000 acres in the county are farmland. Tobacco, wheat, corn, rye, oats, and potatoes are the main crops. Farmers also grow onions, spinach, strawberries, asparagus, and fruits. They raise beef cattle, hogs, dairy cows, goats, chickens, turkeys, and rabbits.

In 1859, William Frego killed a fourteen-month-old hog he had raised that supposedly weighed 413 pounds.   *FUN FACT*

Grapes are grown on the eastern side of the Catoctin Mountains. Several vineyards are near the Monocacy River. The Elk Run Vineyard located in Mt. Airy is at the site of a historic 1750s estate.

Maryland's largest brewery is the Frederick Brewing Company on Wedgewood Boulevard in Frederick.

Fascinating Folks (Past and Present)

Franz Louis Michel was a Swiss explorer who came to the Frederick County area in 1702, looking for land and silver mines. He drew a map showing wildlife of the region.

Jacob and Joseph Weller came from Germany and were two of the earliest settlers in what is now Thurmont. They created a kit for matches. Users would dip the match into a chemical, then strike the match against a piece of sandpaper, causing it to catch fire. These match kits were not popular at first but eventually sold well. The Weller home, called the Match House, still stands in Thurmont.

While the Wellers experimented on their match kits, the Match House caught fire several times.   *NOT-SO-FUN FACT*

John Hanson was one of the earliest leaders in the American colonies. In 1781, he was named the president of the colonies by the Congress Assembled (the governing body of that time).

It is believed that **John van Metre** discovered the south branch of the Potomac River, called Wappotomack, sometime before 1725.

John Thomas Schley built the first house and tavern in Fredericktown in 1746, and it stood until 1853. He was also a schoolteacher. His daughter, **Maria Barbara Schley,** was the first child born in Fredericktown in 1746.

John Baltzell built the mansion on East Church Street in Frederick that is now the Historical Society of Frederick County.

James (no last name) was Frederick's first black hero in the American Revolution. He is known to have risked his life spying on the British. He is shown in a painting featuring the Marquis de Lafayette, which hangs in the Historical Society.

Francis Scott Key was born at Pipe Creek near Emmitsburg in 1779. His family lived in a manor house called Terra Rubra. He was well known as a lawyer and a poet. During the War of 1812 at the British bombardment of Baltimore, he wrote the poem that became the "Star-Spangled Banner." He originally called his poem "The Defense of Fort McHenry." He died in 1843 and is buried in the Mt. Olivet Cemetery in Frederick.

Thomas Johnson lived in Frederick at Rose Hill Manor. He was the first Maryland governor elected under the Constitution of 1776. Afterwards, President Washington appointed him to the U.S. Supreme Court. At the death of President Washington, Johnson delivered the eulogy at a memorial funeral procession in Frederick.

Dr. John Tyler lived in Frederick and practiced medicine there. He is recognized as the first doctor to perform cataract surgery in America. He performed the operation in 1763.

In 1917, **William Tyler Page** wrote the American Creed, a statement of belief and duty for citizens of the United States.

Roger Brook Taney became attorney general and later secretary of the treasury of the United States. He became a U.S. Supreme Court justice in 1836. He was the first Catholic named to the Supreme Court. Though born in Calvert County, he moved to Frederick in 1801 and practiced law there. In 1806, he married Ann Key, the sister of Francis Scott Key. Taney gave the oath of office to seven United States presidents, from Martin Van Buren to Abraham Lincoln. He was involved in the Dred Scott Decision, which said that since slaves were not American citizens, they did not have the right to sue in federal courts. Taney died in 1864 and is buried in St. John's Catholic Cemetery in Frederick.

One of the first photography studios in Maryland was opened in 1842 by **Jacob Byerly** in Frederick. The pictures taken at that time were called daguerreotypes. They were made using copper plates covered with silver and treated with iodine vapor. Eventually the business passed to Byerly's son and then to his grandson. The three men took thousands of pictures of people, buildings, and historic events that took place in the county. This was important because most of those pictures have survived and show us what life was like at that time.

Daguerreotype photography was very slow. People who were having a picture taken had to sit perfectly still for fifteen to twenty minutes.   *FUN FACT*

Old Wise was a man who lived in a cabin near South Mountain during the Civil War. He was hired by the U. S. government to bury bodies after the Battle of South Mountain. He received one dollar for each body he buried.

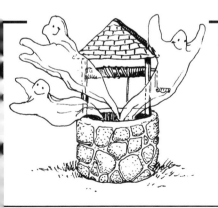

Legend has it that Old Wise got tired of burying bodies and threw seventy-five of them down a well. The ghosts of these men did not like this, and they began to haunt the area. One of the ghosts supposedly confronted Old Wise, who found the man's body and reburied it properly. Actually, Union soldiers had thrown the bodies down the well. Fifty-eight of the bodies were later recovered. Only the foundation of Old Wise's cabin is left.   *NOT-SO-FUN FACT*

Hood College is named for **Margaret Scholl Hood,** who was born in 1833. She was a large contributor to Hood College in its early days. She wanted the college to buy new land and to plan for new buildings. She was very interested in young people. She died July 12, 1913, and was buried in Mt. Olivet Cemetery in Frederick.

Mother Elizabeth Seton (1774–1821) is Maryland's only saint and the first American-born Roman Catholic saint. She is buried near Emmitsburg on the grounds of St. Joseph's College (which closed in 1973). Mother Seton started a school for girls there in 1809. It was called St. Joseph's College. She also started a religious community called the Daughters of Charity. In September 1975, she was canonized (officially made a saint).

Charles Ernest Keller, also known as Charlie "King Kong" Keller, was a major league baseball player. He spent most of his career playing for the New York Yankees in the 1930s and 1940s. He played in four World Series games with a batting average of .306. Keller was born in Middletown and died in Frederick in 1990. A monument was dedicated to him in the fall of 1998. Charlie Keller did not like the nickname "King Kong."

Claire McCardell was a nationally known fashion designer born in Frederick. Her designs were famous in the 1950s.

In 1885, **Theophilus A. Thompson** was the first African-American to be recognized as a chess expert.

Joe Walling, known as "Uncle Joe," made at least five trips across the United States in the early 1900s. On one of these, he walked from Baltimore to San Francisco. He earned money for these trips by selling postcards showing his picture. He worked at many jobs, including wagon-train guide, cowboy, soldier, sailor, telephone lineman, and volunteer fireman. He was from Frederick. He died in 1944.

Blanch Bourne was born in 1917 and became the first woman doctor in Frederick. Her father was also a doctor in Frederick.

Challedon was one of the most famous race horses of his time. He is the only horse who has won two Pimlico Specials. He was Horse of the Year in 1939, and he won $184,353 for Glade Valley Farms near Walkersville.

The **Frederick Keys,** a Class A baseball team, is based in Frederick. The team played its first game in 1989 at McCurdy Field. They moved to Harry Grove Stadium when it was finished in 1990. Many Keys players have become major league players, including Arthur Rhodes and David Segui. Players from the Orioles—Mike Devereaux, Billy Ripken, and Brady Anderson—all have played with the team while recovering from injuries. Pitcher Ben McDonald pitched his first professional game with the Keys in 1989.

Frederick County has many artists and artisans such as painters **Harry and Barry Richardson** and potters **Bill Van Gilder** and **Jan Richardson.**

Natural Resources

In 1772, copper was discovered in Maryland. The first mines to open were located in Frederick and Carroll counties. In Frederick County, the New London Copper Mine opened in 1837. Some years, the mining was very successful and other years, the quarry was open but no ore was mined. The mine was closed in 1904. (Deposits of iron and minerals were also found in Frederick County.)

The greatest amount of copper ore was produced by the Baltimore County copper mines. When larger copper deposits were found further west, Maryland copper mines began to close. Most of them were closed by 1890.

The soil of Frederick County is particularly fertile. This is the most agriculturally productive area in the state. The soil is primarily composed of limestone with some flint and slate. There is also an abundance of red soil, which gets its color from iron.

A special kind of swamp is found in the Catoctin Mountains of Frederick County. In these swamps, water seeps to the surface. No one has disturbed these areas for a long time, and they support many of the state's endangered plants.

Many creeks and rivers in the county provide recreation and beautiful scenery. The Potomac River runs along the southern boundary of the county.

Places of Interest

The **Historical Society of Frederick County** on East Church Street in Frederick was originally a large home built in the 1820s by Dr. John Baltzell.

FUN FACT	At the time Dr. Baltzell built his house, he was in love with a girl from Baltimore. She was not sure she wanted to live forty miles away from her family. In those days, Frederick was still considered the frontier. However, when she saw the beautiful house Baltzell had built, she decided to marry him.

Several other families lived in the home over the years. The last owner, John Loats, donated the building for use as the Loats Female Orphan Asylum in 1879. (The word asylum in this case means refuge.) The orphanage opened in 1882 and was used as a girls' orphanage for about seventy years. Girls lived there until the age of eighteen. After it closed, some people wanted to tear the building down and build a parking lot, but the historical society bought it and now uses it as its headquarters.

The **Barbara Fritchie House and Museum** is located in Frederick. The house, a reproduction of the original, honors Barbara Fritchie, made famous by John Greenleaf Whittier's poem.

Community Bridge spans Carroll Creek in Frederick. In 1994, a work of art was begun that would transform the plain concrete bridge. Pictures of stones and other three-dimensional objects were painted on the bridge. They fool the eye so the viewer thinks the bridge is made of stone and decorated with statues and medallions (pictures painted in round shapes). This form of art is called *trompe l'oeil,* a French term which means "that which deceives the eye." The artist, William M. Cochran, is from Howard County. He and his team worked for four years to complete the entire mural on the bridge.

The bridge was named Community Bridge because everyone in Frederick County, including every elementary school student, was asked to suggest ideas that represented community spirit. The best ideas would be painted on the bridge. Many things were suggested by more than one person. The pictures in the medallions show the ideas suggested by the most people.

Fort Detrick in Frederick was originally an airfield. In 1929, it was leased to the U.S. government to be used as a training camp. In 1943, it was named Camp Detrick after a flight surgeon, Dr. Frederick Louis Detrick, from Frederick. In 1941, research in biological warfare (using disease germs as weapons) was secretly begun at the camp. This was done because Adolph Hitler was thought to be doing the same type of research in Germany during World War II. (The biological warfare research at Fort Detrick ended in 1969.) In 1956, the name was changed to Fort Detrick and it became a permanent army base. In 1972, the fort also became a medical research facility for cancer and infectious diseases. Scientists from Russia have visited the fort to share information about deadly diseases such as plague and anthrax. Scientists hope to develop a vaccine to prevent such diseases so they cannot ever be used as weapons.

Huge dish antennas are located on the grounds of Fort Detrick. These belong to the East Coast Telecommunications Center and the Detrick Earth Station. This communications center is one of the most important in the U.S. Defense Communications System. It is used by the U.S. government and by NATO (the North Atlantic Treaty Organization) to communicate with Russia and other countries around the world.

Camp David is a place for America's presidents, their families, and guests to relax. It is called a retreat, and is located near the town of Thurmont in a forested area of 10,000 acres owned by the U.S. government. The camp itself covers 134 acres. Formerly, Camp David was a fishing camp, built in the late 1930s for $60,000 by the Civilian Conservation Corps as part of the Catoctin recreational demonstration area. The main lodge, called Aspen, was created by connecting four cabins.

Sixty-five feet under the ground is a bomb shelter built during the time when Dwight D. Eisenhower was president.

Camp David is closely guarded to protect the president. The site for the presidential retreat was selected by Franklin Roosevelt. He chose that spot because it was less than seventy miles from Washington, D.C. Roosevelt called it Camp Shangri-La. When Harry S. Truman was president, it was referred to as the summer White House. Soon after he became president in 1953, Eisenhower changed the name to Camp David to honor his grandson David. Many world leaders have met there, including Winston Churchill from England, Premier Nikita Khrushchev from Russia, Prime Minister Menachem Begin of Israel, and President Anwar al-Sadat of Egypt.

The Hessian Barracks are located on the grounds of the first Maryland School for the Deaf in Frederick. They were built by Abraham Faw in 1777 soon after the Revolutionary War started. They housed troops stationed in Frederick. Ammunition was stored there. They also housed Hessian (German) soldiers captured at the battles of Bennington, Saratoga, and Yorktown. From 1853 to 1860, the Frederick County Agricultural Society Fairs were held there. During the Civil War, the barracks were used to house the First Maryland Regiment of the Potomac Home Brigade. They were also used as a Union military hospital. In 1867, the state of Maryland took over the barracks, and in 1868, the Maryland School for the Deaf was opened there.

FUN FACT   The Lewis and Clark expedition was organized at the Hessian Barracks in 1803.

The **Francis Scott Key Monument** in the Mt. Olivet Cemetery in Frederick was dedicated on August 9, 1898. It honors the man who wrote the poem that became the "Star-Spangled Banner," America's National Anthem.

Schifferstadt is the oldest building in Frederick. It is located on the corner of Second Street and Rosemont Avenue and has walls that are 2½ feet thick. Schifferstadt was completed in 1756 by Joseph Brunner, a German immigrant. At one time, it featured a tunnel that ran from the house to the creek so the owners could get water and avoid being attacked by natives in the area. Today it is an architectural museum.

The **Frederick City Hall** is the last of three buildings that stood on or near this site and served as courthouses. The first one was a wooden structure built in 1750. From this building, the Stamp Act was repudiated, and seven Tories (British sympathizers in the American Revolution) were sentenced to be hanged. When the wooden courthouse began to rot, a new courthouse was authorized in 1784 and built in 1787. It burned in May 1861. Another courthouse was built that same year, remodeled in 1954, and again remodeled and restored in 1985. Yet another courthouse was built on Patrick Street in the early 1980s, and the old courthouse was not used for about a year. In 1983, the mayor and board of aldermen authorized the purchase of the old building to be used as the City Hall.

Baker Park is a large park in the city of Frederick. It is enjoyed by residents and visitors alike. At one time, a 100-foot iron and wood "swinging bridge" was located in the park, but it has been torn down because of safety concerns.

The **Brunswick Railroad Museum,** located in the town of Brunswick, depicts railroading in the early 1900s. In addition to the exhibits and artifacts, the museum has a model railroad. Also in Brunswick is a restored train station built in 1891.

The **National Shrine of St. Elizabeth Ann Seton,** located in Emmitsburg, honors the first American-born Catholic canonized (declared a saint) by the church (1975). Seton established the first Catholic school in America in 1810.

The **National Shrine Grotto of Lourdes** is a replica of the famous Grotto of Lourdes in France. It was the first Catholic shrine in the United States and the oldest replica of the Grotto of Lourdes in the Western Hemisphere. It is located on a mountainside above Mt. St. Mary's College near Emmitsburg. A large golden statue of the Virgin Mary is at the site.

The **National Museum of Civil War Medicine** is located on East Patrick Street in Frederick. It is housed in a building that was used to embalm (prepare for burial) those who had died at the Battle of Antietam. The museum focuses on the importance of the Civil War to the development of medicine and the way it is practiced today. Visitors can see a camp scene with the doctor's tent and medical equipment. There are also scenes of various other places like barns where the doctors operated.

Rose Hill Manor in Frederick was built in the 1790s by Major John Colin Graham. It was the last home of Thomas Johnson, Maryland's first governor, who served from 1798 to 1819. It is now the **Children's Museum of Rose Hill Manor.** It features hands-on tours for children. It has gardens, a log cabin, a carriage collection, a blacksmith shop, and an icehouse. A farm museum is also on the property.

Carrollton Manor, located west of Buckeystown, was built by Charles Carroll of Carrollton. He did not spend much time there due to his commitment to the cause of freedom in the colonies. The building is not open to the public.

Lily Pons Water Gardens in Buckeystown is named after an opera singer. It has acres of ponds featuring waterlilies and goldfish. Wild birds, beautiful gardens, and wetlands can also be seen.

The **Catoctin Furnace** opened in 1776. It was founded by Thomas Johnson, the first governor of Maryland, and operated until 1903. It produced kettles, pots, and stoves for use in homes. It also made cannons and cannonballs for Washington's Continental Army during the American Revolution. Today, nothing from the original furnace remains above ground. However, stone foundations from buildings of later furnaces can be seen at the site, located off Route 15 between Frederick and Thurmont. A legend states that plates for the Civil War ship *Monitor* were made from pig iron processed at this furnace, but there is no basis for this story since the ship was actually built in New York.

NOT-SO-FUN FACT	The Catoctin Furnace and other industries in the area used an enormous number of trees. By the 1930s, the surrounding mountains were almost bare. The bark was also used by the tanneries, and many trees were cut down for telephone and telegraph poles. Some of the area was replanted.

The **Catoctin Wildlife Preserve and Zoo,** located on U.S. Route 15 in Thurmont, consists of 26 acres of land with a zoo that houses three hundred animals. It features interactive shows where audience members can learn about snakes. One of the snakes, Rocky, is a six-foot-long Columbian boa constrictor.

Jug Bridge was built across the Monocacy River in 1807 as part of Frederick Road. It was called Jug Bridge because of a large stone jug on the eastern end of the bridge. The bridge collapsed into the river in 1942.

Legend has it that sealed inside the jug is a bottle of whiskey. The jug is now on display on Bowman Road near Route 70 close to Frederick.

FUN FACT

Monocacy National Battlefield south of Frederick is a Civil War battlefield where Union General Lew Wallace delayed the advances of Confederate General Jubal Early's troops on July 9, 1864. In doing so, he and his troops saved the capital, Washington, D.C., from capture. Monuments can be seen along Urbana Pike and Araby Church Road. The Visitor's Center is open from Wednesday to Sunday. Visitors can also see artifacts and an electronic map of the battlefield.

War Correspondents Memorial is in Gathland Sate Park near Burkittsville. Built by George Alfred Townsend to honor fellow journalists (reporters) who covered the Civil War, it opened in 1896. In 1904, Townsend donated the memorial to the state of Maryland.

The National Fallen Firefighters Memorial is located at the **National Fire Academy** in Emmitsburg. This is the official national memorial to honor firefighters who died in the line of duty.

The Maryland Sheriffs' Youth Ranch in Buckeystown is a school for disadvantaged teenage boys. The ranch offers educational facilities, career development opportunities, and recreational activities to help the boys become more productive members of society. The ranch receives no state or federal funding for buildings or renovations. It is supported by Maryland citizens.

Three historic covered bridges are located in Frederick County. They are **Roddy Road Covered Bridge** near Thurmont, **Utica Mills Covered Bridge** on Utica Road near the town of Thurmont, and **Loy's Station Covered Bridge** on Old Frederick Road.

Parks and Recreational Areas

The Appalachian Trail is a hiking trail that runs from Maine to Georgia through some of the most scenic countryside on the East Coast. Forty-one miles of this beautiful trail run through Maryland on the crest of South Mountain.

In 1930, J. Frank Schairer was hired to design the section of the trail that would pass through Maryland. He had to be sure the route would connect with the Pennsylvania and West Virginia trails, which had been planned earlier. He decided the best route would be along South Mountain. Over a period of four days, two foresters, F. W. Besley and Cyril Klein, blazed the trail, marking trees to designate the route. Then the members of the Potomac Appalachian Trail Club cleared the trail so it would be easy to walk. Today ten overseers maintain the Maryland section of the trail, cutting back the vines, weeds, and small bushes.

Cunningham Falls State Park is located near Thurmont. The highlight of this park is Cunningham Falls, the highest in Maryland. It has a 78-foot waterfall in a rocky gorge. The park also features a 43-acre lake. The entire park covers 4,946 acres and is divided into two distinct recreational areas. These are the Manor area and the William Houck area. Visitors can camp and hike the many trails, or go boating, swimming, fishing, hunting, and cross-country skiing.

Gambrill State Park is located six miles northwest of the city of Frederick. It features fishing, camping, picnicking, cross-country skiing, and hiking. It has many scenic overlooks. The park covers 1,137 acres.

Gathland State Park near Burkittsville spans both Frederick and Washington counties. George Alfred Townsend, a Civil War journalist, once lived there. He designed and built many of the buildings. Visitors can see a large, stone monument that is dedicated to war correspondents. They can also enjoy picnicking, hiking, and cross-country skiing. The park is 140 acres in size.

Sugarloaf Mountain, near the southern boundary of the county, was so named because it looked like an old-fashioned loaf of sugar to the early settlers rowing up the Potomac River. A sugarloaf was a cone-shaped mass of crystallized sugar. In 1902, a man named Gordon

Strong saw Sugarloaf Mountain and began buying land in the area. He eventually acquired 2,000 acres. He turned them into a scenic attraction that includes a mansion called Stronghold. The area now draws thousands of visitors a year.

It took about fourteen million years for the surrounding land to erode, leaving Sugarloaf Mountain.	*FUN FACT*

The **C&O Canal and Towpath** is a part of the Chesapeake and Ohio Canal that runs from Washington, D.C., to Cumberland following the Potomac River. The canal is a National Historic Park. Visitors can enjoy camping, picnicking, hiking, skating, and cycling.

Catoctin Mountain National Park is a 6,000-acre park featuring hiking trails, scenic drives, campsites, and picnic facilities. It is located on Maryland Route 77 west of Thurmont. The Spicebush Nature Trail was developed specifically for visitors with disabilities.

CHAPTER 10

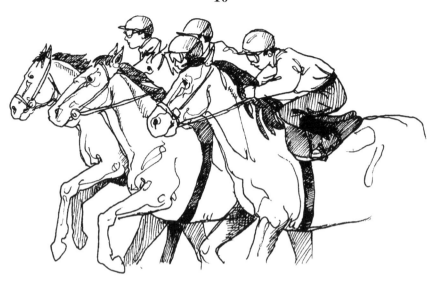

HARFORD COUNTY (1773)

Harford County is one of Maryland's fastest growing counties. Its farmland is gradually disappearing as development continues to increase. However, the county has managed to maintain much of its rural beauty.

By the 1990 census, 182,132 people lived in the county. It is estimated there will be 231,400 by the year 2010.

Establishment of the County

Harford County was once part of Baltimore County, which originally covered a very large area. In the early 1770s, people living in the area around Bush River and the Chesapeake Bay disliked the long trip to Baltimore Town. It was the county seat at that time. People needed to travel there to serve on juries and conduct business. In 1773, the people petitioned the Maryland General Assembly to divide Baltimore County. The Assembly then passed the act that allowed Harford County to be separated from Baltimore County. Aquila Hall, Benedict Edward

Hall, John Hall of Cranberry, Amos Garrett, Richard Dallam, John Matthews, and John Paca were named as the first commissioners of Harford County.

The new county was named after Henry Harford, the illegitimate son of the sixth Lord Baltimore. Harford did not show much interest in his land, but probably visited several times. He lost the land in 1780 when the Maryland Legislature passed a law prohibiting British subjects from owning land in the state. Maryland paid Harford 10,000 pounds (about $16,000) for the land. Later, Henry Harford spent time in a British prison for not paying his debts.

NOT-SO-FUN FACT

County Seat

Harford County has had two county seats: Harford Town (now Bush), 1773–1782; and Scott's Old Fields (now Bel Air), 1782 to today.

When Harford was officially established as a separate county in 1773, it was decided that the center of government would be located at the place where Routes 7 and 136 intersect today. The town of Bush (or Harford Town) had a tavern, tannery, stagecoach house, hotel, gristmill, several inns, and twenty to forty homes. No courthouse was ever built. It is thought that court was held in a warehouse owned by a man named Webster. It was known as the "Brick Storehouse."

There was no jail in Bush, so a room in a local building was rented to house prisoners. *FUN FACT*

In spite of the historic events that took place at Bush before the Revolutionary War, it was the county seat for only nine years. Just two buildings are left today from the original Harford Town or Bush.

Bel Air had its beginnings in 1780 when a man named Aquilla Scott laid out a town on a portion of his plantation, Scott's Improvement. The town had forty-two lots and was called Scott's Old Fields. Some lots were bought by an innkeeper, a tavern keeper, several attorneys, merchants, and county officials. In about twenty years, the town also had a number of craftsmen, a Methodist meetinghouse, and the courthouse. It became the new county seat in 1782 and was renamed Belle Air in 1783. It was one of five towns being considered. People wanted their government to be more centrally located in the county than Bush. By 1786, the name was changed to Bel Air on court records, though some people continued to use the old spelling. In 1874, Bel Air was incorporated as a town. A board of five commissioners was elected.

The first courthouse, a beautiful colonial-style building, was built in 1791. The courthouse burned in 1858, and the present courthouse was built soon after. Several additions enlarged the building.

Growth in the Twentieth Century

In the early 1900s, most of Harford County consisted of farming communities. At that time, Bel Air, Havre de Grace, and Aberdeen were the largest towns. By the 1940s, population had increased, creating a demand for more and better schools. During this time, some of the greatest changes took place in Harford County schools. By 1947, $4 million was borrowed by the county to build them. Curriculum was modernized and more schools were consolidated (combined).

Services for citizens improved as the county became more urban. General stores, which once boasted they sold everything, began to close. They were replaced by specialty markets such as hardware stores, drug stores, clothing stores, and supermarkets. This growth continued into the 1990s, when people began to protest the ongoing development in the county. They were upset about the loss of farmland, increased traffic congestion, and overcrowding in the schools.

County Government

Harford County's government was formed in Bush in 1773 by authority of Henry Harford who was Lord Proprietor. Bush (Harford Town) was the county seat then. The leaders were justices of the court. Although not educated as lawyers, they operated the same way as a court. They tried civil and criminal cases. These justices also collected and distributed taxes, and they acted as overseers for the maintenance of roads, bridges, and county buildings.

During the early 1800s, a board of county commissioners took over governmental tasks such as taxation and management of the county—jobs that had been handled by the justices. The county seat was now Belle Air. Election districts were established. County commissioners, clerks of court, and others were elected instead of being appointed by the governor, General Assembly, or justices.

Today Harford County has a charter government, which was established in 1972 by election. This made Harford the seventh county in Maryland to adopt this form of government. It gives the county more authority than did the county commissioner form of government. In the charter, Harford County's leading office is that of an elected county executive. The legislative branch of the county's government is the county council. There are seven council members, one of whom acts as president. All are elected and they meet once a week.

Major Towns

Three incorporated towns are in the county—Bel Air, Aberdeen, and Havre de Grace. "Incorporated" means that the town leaders (the mayors and city councils or commissioners) have legal rights to conduct business for the town. These towns also have their own police departments.

Bel Air is the largest town in the county as well as the seat of government. In the early 1900s, Bel Air had a race track. The Bel Air Race Track was located on the site of the current Harford Mall and has the distinction of being mentioned in the movie *The Sting*.

In its early times, the railroad was a major contributor to the growth of the town of **Aberdeen.** More important to the town today is its location along Interstate 95 and its closeness to the Aberdeen Proving Ground. The town started at Hall's Cross Roads, a junction of the Old Post Road and a road leading to Bush River Neck. By 1800, there was an inn, a store, and a blacksmith's shop as well as some houses in the town.

FUN FACT

It is believed Aberdeen got its name from a man named Winston from Aberdeen, Scotland. He was the first station agent for the Philadelphia, Wilmington, and Baltimore Railroad for the area. He conducted business from his house and received permission to name the station after his home town of Aberdeen.

In 1852, Edmund Law Rogers designed a village that took the name of the train station, Aberdeen. Two other early towns were incorporated into Aberdeen. They were Hall's Cross Roads and Mechanicsville.

Havre de Grace is a quaint old riverside town located where the mouth of the Susquehanna River meets the Chesapeake Bay. It was incorporated as a town in 1785.

FUN FACT	Along with other towns, Havre de Grace was once considered as a candidate for the capital of the United States.

Havre de Grace had a very successful racetrack. It opened August 24, 1912, with an admission price of one dollar. Famous horses like Man O'War, Citation, and War Admiral raced there. It closed in 1950.

FUN FACT	The first movie theater in Harford County was in Havre de Grace. It was called The Willow.

In the past, the town of **Madonna** has been known as King's Corner, Briar Ridge, and Cathcart. The name Madonna came from a postmaster who named the post office after his daughter.

Abingdon is one of Harford County's oldest towns. It was named for a town in Berkshire, England. It was once a center of industry and manufacturing. Abingdon was originally owned by the Paca family who developed it. Many prominent citizens lived there, including William Paca, a signer of the Declaration of Independence. Cokesbury, the first Methodist college in America, was built there in 1785. The first county newspaper, the *Abingdon Patriot,* and the first silk hat factory in America were located there. Abingdon is one of the fastest developing communities in the county.

Joppatowne, a planned town, was developed in the late 1960s. It is located on the former site of Joppa, one of Baltimore County's earliest county seats.

Jarrettsville was once called Carmen. The name Jarrettsville was a post office name assigned by Luther Jarrett in 1838. Jarrett built a home in 1842 called Jarrett Manor. Jarrett served several terms in the state legislature.

Edgewood was so named because of its location near the edge of the woods in the area. It is the site of Edgewood Arsenal.

Forest Hill began as an agricultural area. With the development of the Ma and Pa Railroad in the 1880s, it became a major milk shipping center.

Churchville was originally called Lower Crossroads, then Herbert's Crossroads. In 1825, the Churchville Presbyterian Church was incorporated and the area was renamed Churchville after the church.

Little is known about how **Darlington** got its name. Some believe it originated from the Darlington family who once lived there. Others believe it was named after a town in northern England. Darlington was home to the Susquehanna Power and Paper Company, in its time a multimillion dollar company.

Churches and Religion

Religious freedom was one of the main reasons people left Europe to settle in the New World. When they arrived, they found others with the same religious beliefs, and they started churches and meetinghouses. In the beginning, they probably met in homes or at a cleared area outside. As soon as they could, they built churches in which to worship. The first church in Harford County served St. George's Parish. This was an Anglican Protestant Episcopal church started by followers of the Church of England sometime between 1671 and 1681. It was used for about forty years. Then people moved farther north and decided to build a new church at Perryman. The present Spesutia Episcopal Church was built in 1851. This church is known as the "Mother of Churches" because several other churches grew from its congregation.

The Quakers have always been an important religious group in the county. Also called Friends, the Quakers had meetinghouses as early as the 1700s. Quakers were active in the Underground Railroad before the Civil War.

Churches and temples in the county now are Apostolic, Baptist, Assembly of God, Catholic, Jehovah's Witness, Lutheran, Methodist, Presbyterian, and Jewish. There are also ethnic religions in the county such as those of the Koreans and Japanese.

Education and Schools

The early settlers had no schools. Those children who received any education at all were taught at home. Wealthier students were sent to schools in Europe or later, in New England.

The first schools were started by the churches in the early 1700s. Some schools hired a teacher for "meat and meals." Some were taught by the pastor. Eventually, people started private schools that accepted pupils who could pay for their education. Teachers were usually men. Their pay was very low. School desks were wooden benches. There were no blackboards. Paper was very expensive and difficult to obtain so students wrote on slates. Penmanship was considered very important, and it was very fancy. The children also learned to read and to "cipher" (do math). In some of the better schools, the students learned Latin, French, and music.

Public schools were authorized by the state constitution of 1876, but there were some public schools even before that. Harford County was divided into school districts in about 1825. Collectors were appointed to raise money for books, school desks, and other things needed. Many one-room schools were established. By the late 1800s, there were about a hundred of these schools. After the Civil War, separate schools were built for black students. The first three in Harford County were built by the Freedman's Bureau, established by an act of Congress in 1865. Eventually, the federal government stopped providing funds, and the schools for black children were operated by the school board. After that, more were built with tax money.

FUN FACT   In 1897, two schools for black children were built. The one at Abingdon cost $250. In contrast, the Abingdon Elementary School, which opened in 1992, cost $5,580,200.

The one-room schools around the county gradually began to disappear as schools were consolidated into larger schools with more rooms. Separate high schools were built for black students and white students. The black schools received "hand-me-down" books and materials from the white schools. Schools were supposed to be separate but equal. In reality, they weren't.

In 1954, the Supreme Court ruled on a landmark case for education. In the case *Brown vs. Board of Education of Topeka, Kansas,* the court said it was unconstitutional to have separate schools for black students. The Superintendent of Schools of Harford County at that time was Charles W. Willis. Integration of elementary schools (black children and white children attending the same school) took place over a two-year period. Integration of high schools was done one grade per year from 1957 to 1963. Black students could choose not to attend integrated schools until 1965. All schools remained open, and the county experienced none of the anti-integration picketing that was going on in other places. However, black leaders did go to court twice to speed up the process.

The population of Harford County continued to grow and new schools were built to serve all of Harford's children.

The county also has several fine private schools, such as St. Margaret's, John Carroll High School, Harford Christian School, Mountain Christian School, Harford Day School, and St. Joan of Arc School.

Harford Community College was founded in 1957. HCC offers a two-year Associate of Arts degree as well as certificate programs (classes relating to only one subject are studied). The school also offers classes relating to hobbies and other interests of people around the county. It boasts the very fine Phoenix Festival Theater, which hosts plays, puppet shows, ballets, and concerts. In 1995, the college opened the Higher Education and Applied Technology Center (HEAT Center) where a number of colleges offer courses.

Businesses, Industries, and Agriculture

Harford County has some important old and new businesses and industries. Harford Mutual Insurance Company in Bel Air was established in 1842 as the Mutual Fire Insurance Company. It is now a nationwide company. The Bata Shoe Company has made shoes since 1939. It was once the largest private employer in the county.

The largest employers in the county today are the Aberdeen Proving Ground and the Edgewood Arsenal. The Upper Chesapeake Health System is the largest private employer. Other large employers are ConStar (Crown, Cork, and Seal), Mercedes Benz, Clorox, the Gap, and Frito-Lay. Another large employer is the Harford County Public School system.

Klein's, Giant Food, Super Fresh, Mars, and others give the people of Harford County a variety of food choices. A farmers market is held in Bel Air during the summer, so people can buy food directly from the farmers. The Harford Mall, Tollgate Plaza, Joppatowne Plaza, The Festival, Beard's Hill Plaza, and other shopping centers give the county an excellent variety of stores. There are department stores such as Montgomery Ward and Hecht's and many fine small businesses.

Other industries relate to three of Harford County's natural resources—the logging of timber and the mining of sand and gravel.

By the late 1800s, Aberdeen was an important shipping point (by railroad) for milk, farm products, and cannery products. Hogsheads (large barrels) of tobacco were brought in from farms in Maryland and Pennsylvania and shipped by water. The dock was on what is now Proving Ground property. Aberdeen was also an important center in the canning industry that was started by the George T. Baker family.

Today, Harford farms supply milk, strawberries, corn, peaches, apples, and other fruits and vegetables.

Fascinating Folks (Past and Present)

Edwin Booth was the brother of John Wilkes Booth, who assassinated President Abraham Lincoln. A fine actor, he performed in both the United States and Europe. He was born at Tudor Hall in Bel Air on November 13, 1833. Edwin Booth died in 1893 and is remembered as one of the greatest Shakespearean actors of all time.

Ira Aldridge was born in Bel Air in 1807. He was another fine Shakespearean actor. He performed in many countries in Europe and was the first black man to be knighted. (In Great Britain, when a man is recognized for some achievement or service to his country, he is given an honor that allows him to use "Sir" before his name.)

Dr. John Archer, 1741–1810, was the first doctor to graduate from a medical school in the United States.

Dr. Archer's graduating class had ten people. He is considered the first to graduate because the diplomas were given in alphabetical order. Since his last name started with A, he was the first to be called.   *FUN FACT*

Dr. Archer and his wife had nine children, and five of them became doctors. Archer opened a medical school in the county. He was a signer of the Bush Declaration and served in the American Revolution. He was also a member of Congress from 1802 to 1808.

Governor William Paca was born in Abingdon in 1704. He was a member of the First and Second Continental Congresses and was a signer of the Declaration of Independence. He was also a chief judge of the Superior Court of Maryland, and he was governor from 1782 to 1785. He died in 1799.

The Rodgers family from the Havre de Grace area boasted numerous military heroes. Among them are **Commodore John Rodgers,** who distinguished himself in the War of 1812, serving as a naval fleet commander. **Commodore John Rodgers II** served in the Seminole War in Florida and in the Civil War. At the time of his death, he was a rear admiral. **Colonel Robert S. Rodgers,** 1809–1891, was a Civil War commander in the army. **Rear Admiral John A. Rodgers,** 1848–1933, and **Commander John Rodgers,** 1881–1926, also served their country and distinguished themselves in the navy.

Captain John Webster, 1789–1877, served in the U.S. Navy for sixty-five years. He was honored by Baltimore City and the State of Maryland for his "gallant defense" of Fort McHenry in Baltimore. He took part in the defense against British ships on September 13, 1814.

Colonel John Streett led the Harford County cavalry in the War of 1812. The town of Street and Street Road are named for his family.

Dr. Howard Kelly was one of the founders of Johns Hopkins Hospital. He lived in Bel Air in his beautiful mansion, Liriodendron, which is used today as a cultural center for Bel Air.

Mayor James Harry Preston served in the Maryland House of Delegates and became its speaker. He also served as police commissioner of Baltimore and was elected mayor of Baltimore in 1911.

Mary Walters Risteau broke ground for women in politics. She was the first woman elected to the Maryland Legislature (1921) and served three terms. She was the first woman elected to the state senate (1935–1937). She was the first woman to serve as Harford County's clerk of court and served as state commissioner of loans. She was appointed as the first woman delegate to the Democratic National Convention in 1936. In addition, she was a successful farmer and lawyer. The district courthouse in Bel Air is named in her honor, the Mary Risteau Building.

Larry MacPhail had an enormous impact on major league baseball. He instituted such things as night baseball, the batting helmet, and season tickets. He was responsible for the first televised baseball game. MacPhail was associated with the Brooklyn Dodgers, the Cincinnati Reds, and the New York Yankees. He owned Glen Angus Farm near Bel Air, and he fought in World Wars I and II.

R. Madison Mitchell earned fame by carving decoys, helping to make Havre de Grace the "decoy capital of the world." From 1901 to 1993, he carved thousands of working and decorative decoys. In 1924, Mitchell began helping Sam Barnes with his decoy business. When Barnes died two years later, Mitchell took over the business.

Mitchell trained many carvers, including **Harry Jobes** and his sons **Bobby, Charlie,** and **Joey; Jimmy Pierce; Patrick Vincenti; Danny Carson; Steve Lay;** and **Linda** and **Dick Robinson.**

Cornelia Meigs was born in Illinois in 1884, but her family home was in Harford County. She was a teacher and author of forty-four books, most written for children. One of them was *Invincible Louisa,* the story of *Little Women* author Louisa May Alcott. This book won the Newbery Award. Meigs died in 1963.

James Warner was a popular photographer who was born in Detroit, Michigan, but lived much of his life in Harford County. He was best known for his photographs of the Amish. He used special filters on his cameras, which made the photos look like paintings.

Scott Garceau, sports anchor for WMAR-TV, channel 2, lives in Fallston.

Cal Ripken, Jr., is one of the Baltimore Orioles all-time star players. His excellence as shortstop and his exceptional batting record ensure Cal a spot in the Baseball Hall of Fame someday. Born in Aberdeen, Cal showed great skill in high school. He played his first big-league game on August 10, 1981, against the Kansas City Royals. His first full season was 1982, when he won the Rookie of the Year Award. On September 6, 1995, Cal broke Lou Gehrig's record of 2,130 consecutive games, and his ovation lasted twenty-two minutes. He ended the streak voluntarily on September 20, 1998, at 2,632 games.

Cal's family has also been active in the Baltimore Orioles. His father, **Cal Ripken, Sr.,** who died in 1999, worked for the organization for years, both as coach and manager. His mother, **Vi Ripken,** cooked after-game snacks for the team. His brother, **Billy Ripken,** also played for the Orioles and other teams.

FUN FACTS

At one time, Cal, Sr., Cal, Jr., and Billy Ripken all worked for the Orioles. Cal, Jr., and Billy played in over six hundred games together as Orioles. Cal was the last major leaguer to bat at Memorial Stadium.

The night Cal tied Lou Gehrig's record and the night he broke it, he changed uniforms after the fifth inning. On the night of game number 2,131, the first uniform went to his son, and the second uniform went to the Ripken Museum in Aberdeen. The museum also has the uniform from game number 2,130.

A bronze statue of Ripken by artist Susan Luery is outside the museum.

Cal, Jr., and his wife Kelly are involved in many community activities. They established the Ripken Learning Center and organized other associations and events that benefit the community. They live in Baltimore County.

Steve Rouse, one of Baltimore's most popular disk jockeys, lives in Fallston. He has the Rouse and Company morning show on WQSR radio. In the many years the show has been on the air, he and his "company," which includes Joppatowne resident, **Maynard G.,** have presented over three thousand morning shows. Rouse also has a popular band called Stevie and the Satellites. They perform in the Baltimore area and have donated more than $120,000 from the sale of CDs to the WQSR Children's Fund. Rouse is also the author of *Rouse and Co. BOOKED.*

Larry McFarland, Marty Ware, Ray Pena, and **Roberto Pena** form the group of international recording artists known as **4 P.M.** McFarland, Ware, and Ray Pena are from Harford County; Roberto Pena is originally from New York, but the group is based in Harford County. They sing *a cappella* (without instrumental backup). Their name, 4 P.M., represents "for positive music." They perform concerts all over the world and give free concerts in schools.

Linda Lowe Morris is a feature writer for the *Baltimore Sun* and is the author of *Morning Milking.* She wrote this book about her experiences growing up on a dairy farm in Harford County. The book was illustrated by **David DeRan,** an artist who also grew up in the county and lived near Linda Lowe Morris. He now lives in Pennsylvania.

Alan R. Cohen is an artist who grew up in Fallston. He is well known for his illustrations in the Chadwick the Crab series of books written by Priscilla Cummings.

Cigar is one of America's most famous racehorses. Born at Country Life Farm in Bel Air in April 1990, he was sold to Allen Paulson of Kentucky. Cigar won many races in his career, but the $3 million Breeders' Cup Classic in 1995 and the $4 million Dubai World Cup (held in the Middle East) were his most famous victories. He was 1995 Horse of the Year. Throughout his career, he won almost $10 million.

Natural Resources

In the past, companies mined chromium and iron from beneath Harford's soil. They also mined serpentine, talc, and iron. Those resources are no longer mined. Today, Harford's major resources are forests, rivers, sand, and gravel.

Logging is a big industry because so many products can be made from wood. Paulownia wood is a lightweight wood that can be carved and worked easily. It is exported to Japan, where it is used for carved boxes and other items. Walnut shells from the county are used for sandblasting the bottoms of ships before they are repainted.

Sand and gravel are mined in the county by a number of companies. They are used in the building industry.

The Susquehanna River flows 444 miles from its head near Cooperstown, New York, through Pennsylvania, and to the Chesapeake Bay at Havre de Grace. It supplies 50 percent of the freshwater that drains into the Bay. The biggest problem for the river (and the Bay) is the water pollution created by the many people who have settled in the area. This is unfortunate, considering over one million people get their water supply from the Susquehanna. The Susquehanna River is the largest of Harford's rivers, but many smaller rivers, streams, and creeks also provide a valuable resource to the county.

Places of Interest

In 1917, a very important event took place in Harford County. By order of President Woodrow Wilson, the federal government took over 35,000 acres of land in southern Harford County for the **Aberdeen Proving Ground** and the **Edgewood Arsenal.** This was a blow to farmers and canneries in the county because all that farmland was lost. The government paid a total of $3,438,000 to land owners in the area. The highest paid was John Cadwalader, who was paid $400,000. Others received less. Food production dropped, but the Proving Ground and Arsenal have been an economic boon to the county since. The thousands of military people stationed there add to Harford's economy. Many civilians are employed there too.

In this case, the word "proving" means testing to make sure a weapon works the way it should. The first testing round was fired on January 2, 1918, in a snowstorm. The Proving Ground is still testing weapons. People living in Aberdeen, Abingdon, Edgewood, and Joppatowne often hear the big booms from the weapons being tested.

The Proving Ground and the Edgewood Arsenal opened in time to make mustard gas (a poison) for soldiers fighting in France during World War I. It was a trying time for the chemists and for commanding officer Colonel William H. Walker, for there were many problems with the production of the deadly gas. In addition, there was an outbreak of the flu, and many people stationed at the Proving Ground died.

Today, the total land and water area used by the Aberdeen Proving Ground and Edgewood Arsenal is approximately 75,000 acres. Weapons of all kinds are developed, tested, and stored there. These are used by the military to defend America's interests around the world. People stationed there have served in World Wars I and II, Korea, Vietnam, and the Persian Gulf War, as well as smaller skirmishes around the world. Since being built in 1917, Aberdeen Proving Ground and Edgewood Arsenal have been vitally important to the security of the United States.

The **Ordnance Museum** on the grounds of the Aberdeen Proving Ground is open to the public. On display is a collection of military artifacts and weapons dating as far back as the American Revolution. Visitors enter along the "mile of tanks" that leads to the museum. The exhibit also includes a 25-acre tank and artillery park with military vehicles, various types of bombs, armored fighting vehicles, and one of the largest collections of military supplies in the world.

The museum is open every day except national holidays. It is open on military holidays such as Veterans Day and Memorial Day.

The **Conowingo Dam** is part of a hydroelectric plant on the Susquehanna River. Built during 1926 and 1927, it was in operation by 1928. At 4,648 feet, it is one of the largest dams in the United States. It has 52 spillway gates, each of which is 22½ feet high and 41 feet wide. They are opened and closed by large cranes. There are seven generators, each of which produces 36,000 kilowatts of electricity. The dam is open for tours, and visitors can go boating and fishing in the lake and river near the dam. Beautiful scenery stretches up and down the river.

The **Ladew Topiary Gardens and Manor House** in Monkton is a fun place to visit because the bushes are trimmed to look like animals. In the front yard, a fox hunt scene is "carved" from bushes. It includes the horsemen, their dogs, and the fox. Many other topiaries can be seen as well. The mansion is also open for tours. This estate was built by Harvey Ladew in the early 1900s. He was an artist who designed the 22 acres of gardens there.

Tudor Hall, near Bel Air, was the home of the Booth family. Two of the sons became famous, Edwin and John Wilkes.

Liriodendron is the beautiful mansion in Bel Air built by Dr. Howard Kelly, who helped found Johns Hopkins Hospital in Baltimore. Exhibits and concerts are held at the mansion.

The **Historical Society of Harford County** is located in the former post office in Bel Air. The society welcomes visitors to view exhibits, find information, and conduct research.

The Hays House in Bel Air is very old. It was built in 1788 and is now operated as a museum by the Historical Society of Harford County.

County Life Farm in Bel Air is Maryland's oldest thoroughbred horse farm. Adolphe Pons established it in 1933, and it has remained in the Pons family ever since. Adolphe Pons handled the sale of Man O'War, one of America's most famous racehorses. The champion racehorse Cigar was born at County Life Farm.

Concord Point Lighthouse in Havre de Grace marks the site of a British attack in the War of 1812. It is one of the oldest lighthouses on the East Coast. The **Havre de Grace Maritime Museum** is nearby.

Poole's Island Lighthouse, built in 1825, is the oldest standing lighthouse in Maryland. Located on the Aberdeen Proving Ground Reservation, it remained in continuous use until 1939.

The **Havre de Grace Decoy Museum** has a wonderful collection of decoys made by some of the state's finest carvers. In addition to the decoys, visitors can see wax figures and photographs of the carvers. At times, carvers are there demonstrating their art.

The **Susquehanna Lockhouse Museum** is located on the Susquehanna River at Havre de Grace. Nearby is the first lock of the Susquehanna and Tidewater Canal. Water levels can be raised or lowered in a lock to help boats go through the canal. Visitors can also see the remains of the canal.

The Promenade in Havre de Grace is a boardwalk along the Chesapeake Bay and Susquehanna River. A marker indicates where these two bodies of water meet.

The **Hosanna Community House** in Darlington was a Freedman's Bureau school for black children. Known as Hosanna School, it was one of three built in the county after the Civil War. It has been restored and is an official Harford County landmark, showing what school was like for black students after the Civil War until 1946. It has been added to the National Register of Historic Places.

The **Fiore Winery** is located on Whiteford Road in Pylesville. Tours are given, and visitors can picnic by the vineyards.

The **Anita C. Leight Estuary Center** is part of the Chesapeake Bay National Estuarine Research Reserve. It is located on Otter Point Creek near Abingdon in southeast Harford County. Its goal is to educate by raising awareness of the estuary. Visitors can see a turtle pond and learn about the marsh habitat. Programs include nature hikes, canoeing, and other family activities.

The **Ripken Museum,** which opened December 6, 1996, is located in Aberdeen at 8 Ripken Plaza. It has many trophies and other memorabilia from Cal Ripken, Jr., and the Ripken family (Cal, Sr., and Billy). Among the trophies is Cal's first Most Valuable Player award from 1983. Visitors can see the bat Cal used in game number 2,131 of his streak and also his uniforms and other items. Many photographs from the Ripken family are on display. Visitors can ask questions of the thirty-six volunteers, and they can watch videos from Cal's career. One video shows the night Cal broke Lou Gehrig's record, and it includes the speech he made that night. Outside the museum is a bronze statue of Cal Ripken, Jr.

Parks and Recreational Areas

Susquehanna State Park is a large park on the banks of the Susquehanna River north of Havre de Grace. Visitors can hike the nature trails, watch the birds, picnic, bicycle, and even fish in the park. Camping is allowed. At the **Steppingstone Museum,** visitors learn about farm life of the past. Demonstrations of arts and crafts of the 1800s are given. Also in the park is the **Archer Mansion,** a thirteen-room home built in 1804. The **Jersey Toll House** is where tolls were collected for the Rock Run Bridge. **Rock Run Grist Mill** is an old gristmill.

Rocks State Park is a beautiful place for picnicking or hiking. It is eight miles north of Bel Air and follows Deer Creek. A gigantic rock formation in the park is called the King and Queen Seats.

Kilgore Falls is the highest waterfall in Harford County and the second
highest vertical waterfall in Maryland.
It is located in the Falling Branch area
of Rocks State Park, 5 miles north of
the main park, and is maintained by
Rocks State Park rangers.

Gunpowder Falls State Park is located along the county line between Harford and Baltimore counties in the Gunpowder River Valley. It is a great place to picnic and hike. The **Jericho Covered
Bridge** (built around 1865) and the **Jerusalem Mill** (1772) are in the
park.

     Mariner Point Park in Joppatowne is a lovely park for picnicking
and hiking along the Gunpowder River.

     Flying Point Park in Edgewood is another pretty place to picnic
and swim. It is on the Bush River.

     Eden Mill Park Nature Center is located on the banks of Deer
Creek in northern Harford County. It was originally called Stansbury
Mill and was part of the estate of Elijah Stansbury, Sr., who built his
home and the mill in 1805. The name Eden is believed to have come
from a Catholic priest, Father Eden, who started a mission nearby. In
the early 1900s, the original mill burned and was replaced by the present building. Harford County has owned the mill and 56 acres of land
since 1965. The Nature Center was established in 1992 and provides
educational and special interest programs. Fishing, canoeing, hiking,
and picnicking are also available.

CHAPTER 11

CARROLL COUNTY (1837)

The rolling countryside of Carroll County continues to be a reminder of its rural past. One of its best-known events is the annual Carroll County 4-H Fair.

In 1995, the population of Carroll County was 140,203. It is projected to reach 178,100 by 2010.

Establishment of the County

As the counties of Frederick and Baltimore continued to grow, it was hard for citizens to travel to the county seats of Frederick and Baltimore Town to conduct business. The roads were muddy when it rained and rutted when it was dry. Several attempts to create a new county failed, but finally in 1833, William C. Johnson of Frederick proposed a new county to be called Carroll County after Charles Carroll of Carrollton. The Maryland General Assembly passed a bill stating that citizens from parts of Baltimore and Frederick counties would vote on this proposal. If the majority from either county opposed the bill, it would not pass.

After much arguing over illegal voting practices, a study was done to see if such a vote was constitutional. It was decided that an amendment would be written by an act of the legislature at one session and it would be passed in its next session. The act was presented to the General Assembly. Governor Thomas W. Veazey supported it, and the act passed on March 25, 1836. On January 19, 1837, the state senate passed the measure and Carroll County was formed.

Carroll County was named after Charles Carroll even though he never lived there.   *FUN FACT*

County Seat

The county seat of Carroll County is Westminster. The town began in 1764, when William Winchester bought 100 acres of land known as White's Level. Instead of naming it after himself, he named it Westminster after his birthplace in England. Over the years, Westminster became a stop for people traveling between Pennsylvania and Baltimore. When people began moving west, Westminster's seven hotels gave them a place to spend the night.

Westminster was chosen as the county seat chiefly through the efforts of Colonel John K. Longwell, founder of the *Carrolltonian*. He had established this paper mainly to bring about the formation of a new county with Westminster as its county seat.

The Carroll County Courthouse located on Court Street was built in 1838 and is still in use today. The courthouse cost $18,000. Today it is known as the historic courthouse. Wings were added about fifty years after the completion of the courthouse. Courtroom number "1" has been called one of the most beautiful courtrooms in America by the American Bar Association. In the 1940s, scenes for the movie *Maryland* were filmed in the courthouse.

The Carroll County Courthouse has been used in several movies. It has the original   *FUN FACT*
benches, jury chairs, desks, and woodwork. There are four brass chandeliers in the
courtroom. James Shellman received $10.00 for designing the courthouse.

Growth in the Twentieth Century

Carroll County has always been mostly rural. However, during the twentieth century, many businesses were established in the towns. Westminster grew during the 1920s, 1930s, and 1940s, serving both the farm community and the townspeople with shops and businesses. On weekends, the town was a gathering place for people to meet and socialize. At that time, parking was a problem because cars were becoming popular, and the towns were unprepared for the traffic.

NOT-SO-FUN FACT	Since people were double-parking in Westminster, the city council voted to install parking meters in 1941. Many people were upset about paying to park. They did not like the modernization of the town.

Trains were losing popularity as people preferred to drive their cars. During the later part of the century, Carroll County built new roads.

The board of education began to improve educational services. Older schools were closed, and plans were made to build modern ones.

In 1964, Eldersburg was designated to be a high-growth area for the next ten years. The area, called the Freedom District, grew so fast that schools, water, and sewage services could not keep pace. Eldersburg, originally a small town, is now a large community of many people who work in other cities and towns.

Towns watched the growth of such businesses as fast-food restaurants and department stores. Shopping centers and malls such as the Cranberry Mall were built. Small grocery stores were replaced by supermarkets. Towns like Westminster now serve as residential communities for people who commute to jobs in Baltimore and Washington.

Sometimes growth can be difficult and can even threaten some species of animals. The bog turtle has been on the endangered species list since 1997. Construction of a bypass around Hampstead was halted so people could decide how to preserve this small turtle.

County Government

The three-member board of county commissioners is elected by the voters for a four-year term. Leading the board are the president, the vice president, and the secretary, all chosen by the board. The commissioners set the budget for the county and executive policies and oversee government agencies. Their offices are located in the county office building at 225 North Center Street in Westminster.

Major Towns

Westminster did not have the characteristics that prompted the growth of most settlements. It had no forts, no natural roads, no rivers or harbors. No people were requesting a town be founded there.

In the early 1800s, Westminster was known as the longest town for its population in America. This was because the town kept expanding along the main highway.

FUN FACT

Uniontown is one of Carroll County's oldest towns. The land, known as the Orchard, was granted on April 6, 1779, to Thomas Metcalf, and the town was built there. Its citizens once petitioned the state to create a new county from Baltimore and Frederick counties and to make Uniontown the county seat. It is believed that its original name was "Forks" because it was located at the intersection of Buffalo Road and the main road from Baltimore to Hagerstown. At the time, this road was an important north-south route. The date when Uniontown officially became a town is unknown. However, land records indicate it began to develop as a town between 1809 and 1811, and was officially surveyed in 1824. Uniontown has changed little since the 1800s.

Manchester was established by English and German settlers in 1760. It was named after the English town of the same name. Manchester became a center for agricultural trade. Tobacco was grown there, and cigars were manufactured in the town after the Civil War.

Sykesville is named after James Sykes, who bought land in the area in 1825 from George Patterson. Mills were built along the south branch of the Patapsco River, which encouraged growth in the area. When the B&O Railroad was built in 1831, Sykesville grew rapidly.

Part of Sykesville was destroyed in the great flood of 1868, when the waters of the Patapsco came raging through.

NOT-SO-FUN FACT

Established in 1754, **Taneytown** is the oldest town in Carroll County. It was named after Raphael Taney who, with Edward Diggs, received a land grant of 7,900 acres. Taney established the town, but he did not live there. He was from St. Mary's County. Taneytown grew up in an area once known as "Maryland's backwoods" though its official name was Brother's Agreement. At one time, it was an important center for the sale of grain and feed for animals. The Taneytown Elevator Company was one of the first grain elevator companies in the country.

FUN FACT	Many people mistakenly think that Taneytown was named after U.S. Supreme Court Chief Justice Roger Brooke Taney. However, it was actually named for Raphael Taney. Roger Brooke Taney was not born until 1777.

The history of the **Mt. Airy** region began when settlements developed along the Old National Pike in the early 1700s. Mt. Airy grew with the building of the B&O Railroad in the early 1830s. In 1839, Mt. Airy became a station on the Old Main Line. It is located close to the intersection of Carroll, Frederick, Howard, and Montgomery counties.

NOT-SO-FUN FACT	Mt. Airy has had many terrible fires during its history. Portions of the town burned three times. Fire destroyed the downtown area in 1903 or 1904, 1914, and 1925. It is believed this occurred because the buildings were built so close to each other along winding streets on steep hillsides.

Hampstead was laid out in 1786 by Christopher Vaughn on land previously known as Spring Garden. It was originally called Coxville after John Cox, who was the first man to settle there. Canning and flour mills were major businesses that contributed to the growth of the town, which was incorporated in 1888.

Francis Scott Key, author of the "Star-Spangled Banner," was born on a farm called Terra Rubra near **Keysville.** The farm was named after the dark reddish-brown soil found in the area.

Union Bridge developed from two small settlements on either side of Little Pipe Creek. Settlers built a bridge across the water and marshland to unite the two towns. They called the combined towns

Union Bridge to reflect their united effort in building the bridge. The town was chartered by the Maryland General Assembly on May 2, 1872.

New Windsor is the smallest of the incorporated towns in Carroll County. It was laid out in 1797 by Isaac Atlee along the old Monocacy wagon road that went from Winchester, Virginia, to Philadelphia. It was incorporated in 1844. The town has a rich religious history dating back to 1758, when the Church of the Brethren was established. The area was popular in the 1790s for the sulfur spring baths. This town is the home of the New Windsor Service Center, known around the world for its disaster relief efforts.

Main Street in New Windsor used to be called Bath Street after the sulfur spring baths.

FUN FACT

Churches and Religion

Freedom of religion lured many groups of people to settle in Maryland. Congregations of Friends (Quakers), Brethren (also known as Dunkards), Reformed, Lutherans, and Methodists were established before 1770.

The first Methodist service in America was held in Carroll County under a large tree called the Strawbridge Oak. (The tree was cut down in 1907. The wood was used to make furniture, some of which is still in existence.) Robert Strawbridge preached under the oak and is considered the first Methodist minister in the United States. Soon after he came to the county, a cabin was built in which to hold services. It was called the Strawbridge Meetinghouse. It was also known as Sam's Creek and Pipe Creek Meetinghouse. Several years later, a new chapel was built, called Poulson's Chapel. In 1944, a very important event happened in the county when Immanuel Methodist and Centenary Methodist Churches joined to form the Westminster United Methodist Church. This is important because Methodism was the county's largest religious group. This merger occurred just before World War II.

The Quakers were holding meetings at the home of the Farquhars, who lived in the place that would become Union Bridge by 1735. The only Quaker meetinghouse in the county was built in the 1770s. The land was donated by William Farquhar.

Members of the Lutheran and Reformed religions worshipped together until after the Civil War, when each built a church. Other churches such as the Catholic, Presbyterian, and Anglican churches were established after 1779.

Today, congregations such as Lutheran, Reformed, Catholic, Episcopal, United Methodist, United Church of Christ, Church of God, Bible Church, Church of Jesus Christ of Latter-Day Saints, and others worship in Carroll County.

Education and Schools

In 1762, the first school in the county was started by the Lutheran and Reformed congregations in Manchester. Another of Carroll County's early schools was the Uniontown Academy, which was established in 1810. It was built to serve as a school for English-speaking students who previously attended German schools. It was open until 1865. Today, it is on the National Register of Historic Places. Before the Civil War, the Uniontown Academy and other schools were supported by churches or other private groups. Other private schools were located in Clover Hill, Deer Park, Oakland, and Westminster. One of the best schools in the area at that time was run by the Quakers at Pipe Creek Meetinghouse. Another early school had been built in Hampstead soon after 1831.

The Board of School Commissioners of Carroll County was established on August 7, 1865.

FUN FACT   The Thorndale Seminary for Young Ladies, which opened in 1837, charged 50¢ per session for the use of the library. There were two sessions each year. The girls paid $110 each session for boarding and tuition. In addition, they paid $25 to learn to play the piano, $10 for drawing and painting lessons, and $10 to learn to speak French.

By 1870, students studied algebra, arithmetic, bookkeeping, geography, grammar, history, philosophy, and writing. Some of the schools had no chalkboards or wall maps.

One-room schools opened in the late 1800s. Emery Chapel School, opened in 1876, was one of the first.

In 1868, plans were made for a school system for "the colored children of the county." Several schools were built soon after, such as Middletown African School and West End African School.

In 1877, applications were made to form "colored" schools in Taneytown and elsewhere. By 1883, Carroll County had seven schools for black students. By 1912, there were 134 one- or two-room schools for white students and 12 for black students. When Maurice H. Unger became county school superintendent in 1916, plans for consolidating the one- and two-room schools began. The last one-room schoolhouse, Oakland Mills, closed in 1953. Deep Run and Harney were the last two-room schools to close in 1956.

During the 1950s and 1960s, schools were gradually desegregated (black students and white students no longer attended different schools). Today, Carroll County's public school students represent a diversity of cultures and races.

Carroll County also has some fine private schools, including Carroll Christian School, Mt. Airy Mennonite School, Montessori School of Westminster, St. John's Catholic Elementary, and Faith Christian School. The Carroll County Outdoor School, The Carroll County Career and Tech Center, and the Gateway School provide other forms of education for Carroll County students.

Carroll Community College is a two-year school. Classes are held at several locations besides the main campus in Westminster.

Western Maryland College was established by Fayette R. Buell in 1866 and began holding classes in 1868. Buell was not from Carroll County, but came to the county to start a school and later a college. The college eventually was administered by the Methodist-Protestant Church. Today it is not associated with any church.

FUN FACT   Western Maryland College was the first college south of the Mason-Dixon Line for both male and female students. Most colleges of that time admitted only boys or only girls.

Businesses, Industries, and Agriculture

By the end of the 1800s, Carroll County's manufacturing industries included paper mills, sawmills, cigarmaking factories, tanneries, canning factories, mines, and a steam-engine factory. A wormseed-oil factory also existed that distilled oil for the production of medicines. At one time, Carroll County was the world's largest wormseed-oil producer.

Technology was also beginning to advance. Oliver Evans invented a machine that automatically processed wheat into flour. This enabled three workers to do work that formerly required eighteen. Stores at this time served many purposes. One of these was the Patapsco Store, which operated as a general store, post office, and railroad station. Many towns had banks and stores selling various products. There were also a number of hotels and inns to accommodate travelers.

Today, Carroll County's major employers include the Board of Education, Random House Publishers, Carroll County General Hospital, Springfield Hospital Center, and Black and Decker.

Because of its fertile land and rolling hills and valleys, agriculture was the most important industry throughout most of Carroll County's history. Before the formation of the county in 1837, the people who settled in the area dealt with poor tools, hard-to-travel roads, scarcity of labor, fungal diseases on the crops, insects, erosion, and wars.

In 1840, the census showed corn as the main product, followed by wheat, oats, and rye. The grains were used to feed livestock.

The world's first reaping machine was invented in 1811 by Jacob R. Thomas, who lived near Union Bridge. His cousin, Obed Hussey, improved the machine and patented it (obtained the exclusive right to make and sell his invention) in 1833. This is important because Cyrus McCormick, who is credited with inventing the reaper, did not patent his until one year later.

Carroll County leads Maryland counties in preserving agricultural land for future generations. It also ranks near the top in the entire United States. Farmers grow grains such as barley, wheat, and corn. They also grow soybeans, hay, strawberries, and a variety of vegetables. They raise sheep, cattle, hogs, and poultry. The dairy industry is also important. The number of farms in Carroll County decreased during the 1980s and 1990s, though the average farm increased in size.

Fascinating Folks (Past and Present)

John K. Longwell was one of the earliest writers to record the history of Carroll County. He wrote *Historical Sketch of Carroll County*. He also bought a newspaper business and began publishing the *Maryland Recorder*. In 1833, he started the *Carrolltonian* which became the *Westminster Carrolltonian*. By 1836, he was commander of the Westminster Riflemen, a military unit. In 1842, he led the Carroll Infantry as captain. His career also included the offices of county commissioner, member of the 1867 state constitutional convention, director of Union National Bank, and president of Baltimore and Reisterstown Turnpike Company. He wrote the charter (the document defining the company's right to operate the business) of Western Maryland Railroad. Longwell Avenue in Westminster is named after him.

Elizabeth (Betsy) Patterson was born in Sykesville in the late 1700s. Her romance with Prince Jerome Bonaparte of France is a combination of fact and fiction. She met the prince at a racetrack in Baltimore. Her father did not want her to see the prince again, so when she was invited to a ball, he locked her in her room. As the story goes, she put on her gown, climbed down a rainspout, rode a mule into Baltimore, and arrived just a little late to the ball. She and the prince were married in 1803. Prince Jerome was the brother of Napoleon Bonaparte, the emperor of France. Napoleon wanted Jerome to marry a member of a royal family from Europe and refused Betsy entry to the country when she arrived in France. Although she had Prince Jerome's son, she never saw the prince again.

Colonel James M. Shellman was the first mayor of Westminster. He was a militia officer, and he designed the Carroll County Courthouse.

William Henry Rinehart, born in Union Bridge in 1825, is one of America's most famous sculptors. His works include the fountain for the Old Post Office in Washington and the bronze doors of the rotunda in the U.S. Capitol. He also designed the bronze doors to the House and Senate wings in the Capitol. Another well-known piece is the sculpture of Chief Justice Roger Brooke Taney in Annapolis. Other sculptures are on display in art museums in Washington, Baltimore, and New York.

Sleepy Hollow, New York, may be famous for its headless horseman, but Keysville has one too. Reportedly, the **Headless Horseman of Keysville** has been seen riding between Sixes Bridge and Keysville on Long Woods Road.

Francis Scott Key, author of the "Star-Spangled Banner," was born at Terra Rubra in Carroll County.

Frank Brown was the only governor of Maryland from Carroll County. His former home, called Springfield, is now Springfield State Hospital.

In 1948, **Whittaker Chambers** claimed that the accused spy Alger Hiss gave him papers and microfilm to be passed on to the Russians. Investigators went to Westminster to Chambers's farm. Chambers led them out into his pumpkin patch. He lifted the top off one of the pumpkins, revealing microfilm and papers hidden there. These items became known as the Pumpkin Papers or the Pumpkin Patch Papers. Chambers testified against Hiss in court. Alger Hiss was not convicted of spying, because the statute of limitations had run out on the espionage charges. He was convicted of perjury (lying under oath). He was sent to prison for five years, but he served only forty-four months. Chambers died in 1961 and was awarded the Medal of Freedom posthumously (after he died) by President Ronald Reagan.

Robert Wyndam Walden was the greatest horse trainer of the nineteenth century. He had a farm in Middleburg called Bowling Brook. He built an octagonally shaped barn with a quarter-mile race track inside so that his horses could train all year. This gave him an advantage over his competitors, and his horses won the greatest number of races. He won $1.3 million in purses. Walden died in 1905.

Fred Gwynn played Herman in the *Munsters* television show, which is still being shown in reruns on cable. He also wrote the children's books *The King Who Rained, A Chocolate Moose for Supper,* and *A Little Pigeon Toad.*

Natural Resources

Carroll County's fertile soil and its many streams, runs, and ponds have contributed greatly to farming, the county's main occupation. Carroll County is also known for the Silver Run limestone that has been mined and used for roads and cement. Wakefield marble is also mined and used for decorative purposes.

The county has beautiful hills, valleys, and forests. Another major natural resource is the Patapsco River, which forms the southern border and separates Carroll from Howard County. A portion of the river flows through the Patapsco Valley State Park.

Places of Interest

The **Carroll County Farm Museum** in Westminster was originally an almshouse (a home for the poor). Today, it is a museum. The house, the craft building, and the barn were built in 1852 and 1853. Visitors can see how a farmer and his family lived at that time. Farm animals, farm tools, crops, colonial crafts, and carriages can also be seen. Special events are held during the year such as Children's Day in May, a Living History Camp in July, Summer Reading Day near the end of summer, and Fall Harvest Days in October.

The Sherman-Fisher-Shellman and Kimmey Houses on East Main Street in Westminster were the homes of leading citizens of the town. Today, they are owned by the **Historical Society of Carroll County.** Visitors can see the famous collection of dolls in the Miss Carroll Dollhouse. Other antique toys are also on display.

The Western Maryland Railway Historical Society Museum located in Union Bridge is a restored Victorian train station.

The **Baltimore and Ohio Railroad Station** at Mt. Airy was in use from 1868 to 1882.

The **New Windsor Service Center** is located in New Windsor. This organization provides clothing, medicine, and other services to needy people around the world. The **International Gift Shop** carries handmade gifts from forty countries.

The Methodist Church in America started in New Windsor. The **Strawbridge Log Meetinghouse** is a replica of the Methodist Meetinghouse built in 1760 when this religion started. It is believed that Robert Strawbridge was the first Methodist preacher in the United States.

City Hall in Westminster was built in 1842 by Colonel John K. Longwell. He lived in this mansion (called Emerald Hill at the time) and became an important figure in Westminster and in the county. The city bought the home in 1939 and converted it to the city hall.

Terra Rubra near Keysville is the birthplace of Francis Scott Key. The estate was established by Philip Key from London, England, who was granted 1,865 acres of land in the early 1700s. The American flag flies there twenty-four hours a day by a special act of Congress.

The **Union Mills Homestead and Grist Mill** is located north of Westminster on Littlestown Pike. It belonged to the Shriver family for six generations. The mill has stone mill wheels, which grind corn and wheat into flour. It was established in 1797 as a business site for David and Andrew Shriver. It became a gristmill and sawmill. The Union Mills Homestead was named because the brothers were in partnership. Eventually, it included a coopershop, a blacksmith, and a tannery. The brothers also built a house. Over the years, it was enlarged from six rooms to twenty-three rooms to provide for Andrew's growing family.

Cold Friday on Bachman Valley Road is the farm where Whittaker Chambers hid papers given to him by accused spy Alger Hiss. The farm is a national historic site.

Three wineries near Mt. Airy have tours: **Elk Run Vineyard** on Liberty Road, **Berrywine Plantations Linganore Winecellars** on Glissans Mill Road, and **Loew Vineyards** on Liberty Road.

The Sykesville Gate House Museum of History on Cooper Drive in Sykesville was originally the residence of the people in charge of the Springfield Hospital Center. Today, it is a museum with exhibits and photographs relating to local mills, farms, banks, and the B&O Railroad. A research library is also located there.

Parks and Recreational Areas

Piney Run Park in Sykesville has 500 acres of woodlands and a 300-acre lake. People can visit the nature center, have a picnic, play tennis, ride bikes, and go boating, fishing, birding, or horseback riding. The park is open from April through October.

At **Cascade Lake** in Hampstead, visitors can have a picnic or go hiking, swimming, and fishing. A playground, water slides, paddle boats, horseshoe pits, an arcade, and a gift shop are also there. A favorite with children is the giant frog sliding board, where they slide down the frog's tongue into the water.

Hashawha Environmental Center near Union Mills has 320 acres. Visitors can camp and swim in the pool.

The Union Mills Reservoir Area is a 1,360-acre site. Activities include hiking, horseback riding, and cross-country skiing.

Carroll County shares **Liberty Reservoir** with Baltimore County. This area near the southeast corner of Carroll County covers 5,897 acres and is a source of water for Baltimore City. The lake offers visitors hiking, boating, and fishing.

At **Freedom Park** in Sykesville, people can hike, have a picnic, or play softball, baseball, or soccer. Youngsters can play at the tot-lot.

The **River Valley Ranch** northeast of Manchester offers camping, horseback riding, picnicking, and swimming.

The **Morgan Run Natural Environment Area** is a 1,300-acre environmental reservation off Route 97 south of Westminster. Hiking the trails provides visitors a wonderful view of the wildlife.

The **Gillis Falls Reservoir Site** is located near Mt. Airy. Visitors can hike the trails and fish in the reservoir.

A portion of **Patapsco Valley State Park** is located in Carroll County. This section of the park, located on the south branch of the Patapsco River, is in the southeastern part of the county.

BIBLIOGRAPHY

Block, Victor, and Fyllios Hockman. *The Pelican Guide to Maryland*, 2nd ed. Gretna, Louisiana: Pelican Publishing Company, 1995.

Brooks, Neal A., and Eric G. Rockel. *A History of Baltimore County*. Towson, Md.: Friends of the Towson Library, 1979.

Brooks, Neal A., and Richard Parsons. *Baltimore County Panorama*. Towson, Md.: Baltimore County Public Library, 1988.

Cannon, Timothy L. *Pictorial History of Frederick, Maryland*. Frederick, Md.: Key Publishing Group, 1995.

Delaplaine, Edward S. *The Origin of Frederick County, Maryland*. Washington: Judd & Detweiler, Inc., 1949.

Goldstein, Louis L. *Louis Goldstein's Maryland*. Annapolis, Md.: Maryland State Archives, 1985.

Historical Society of Harford County. *Harford Historical Bulletin*. Bel Air, Md.: Historical Society of Harford County, quarterly publication.

Jessop, Jennie E. *The Origin of Names in Baltimore County*. Cockeysville, Md.: Baltimore County Historical Society, n.d.

Kalman, Bobbie. *Visiting a Village (Historic Communities Series)*. New York: Crabtree Publishing Co., 1993.

Manakee, Harold R. *Indians of Early Maryland*. Baltimore: Maryland Historical Society, 1959.

Manakee, Harold R. *Maryland in the Civil War*. Baltimore: Pridemark Press (Maryland Historical Society), n.d.

Marck, John T. *Maryland the Seventh State, A History*. Glen Arm, Md.: Creative Impressions, Ltd., 1995.

Maryland Department of Business and Economic Development and the Maryland Department of Housing and Community Development.

Maryland Celebrates History, A Guide to Maryland's Historical Attractions. Baltimore: Maryland Department of Business and Economic Development and the Maryland Department of Housing and Community Development, 1996.

Minnich, Dean L. *Towns and Villages of Carroll County*. Westminster, Md.: Carroll County Chamber of Commerce, 1995.

Nicholson, Lois. *Cal Ripken, Jr., Quiet Hero*. Centreville, Md.: Tidewater Publishers, 1993.

Panek, Susan. *An Overview of Carroll County*. Carroll County, Md.: League of Women Voters, n.d.

Rollo, Vera Foster. *Maryland Today: A Geography*. Lanham, Md.: Maryland Historical Press, 1994.

Rollo, Vera Foster. *Your Maryland: A History*. Lanham, Md.: Maryland Historical Press, 1993.

Schaun, George, and Virginia Schaun. *Biographical Sketches of Maryland*. Annapolis, Md.: Greenberry Publications, 1969.

Scharf, J. Thomas. *History of Western Maryland,* Volume II. Baltimore: Regional Publishing Company, 1968.

Taylor, Colin F., editorial consultant. *The Native Americans, the Indigenous People of North America*. New York: Smithmark Publishers, Inc., 1991.

Warner, Nancy M., et al. *Carroll County, Maryland, A History, 1837–1976*. Westminster, Md.: Carroll County Bicentennial Committee, 1976.

Williams, T. J. C., and Folger McKinsey. *History of Frederick County, Maryland*. Baltimore: Regional Publishing Company, 1967.

Wright, C. Milton. *Our Harford Heritage*. Bel Air: n.p., 1967.

INDEX

Controlled Demolition, Inc., 84
Cooperstown, New York, 127
copper, 105
Corbit, Captain Charles, 49
corduroy roads, 24
Cornwallis, General, 35
Costello, Jamie, 85
Country Life Farm, 126, 129
Country Peddler Show, 64
county government: Baltimore Co., 75; Carroll, 136; Frederick, 95–6; Harford, 116–7
county seat: Baltimore Co., 73–4; Carroll, 134–5; Frederick, 94; Harford, 115–6
courthouse: Baltimore Co., 74; Carroll, 134–5; Frederick, 67, 109; Harford, 116; Old Baltimore, 73; Towson, 74
Cox, John, 136
Coxville, 136
crafts, colonial, 19, 22, 41, 97
Cranberry Hall, 14
Crouse, Nancy, 47
CSX Railroad, 64
Culp's Hill, 45
Cumberland, 26, 27, 29, 99, 113
Cummings, Priscilla, 126
Cunningham, Bruce, 85
Cunningham Falls, 112
Cunningham Falls State Park, 112

Dallam, Richard, 115
D.A.R.E. (Drug Abuse Resistance Education), 69
Darlington, 36, 43, 119, 130
Darlington family, 119
Daughters of Charity, 9, 104
Declaration of Independence, 35, 98, 118, 123
Declaration of Resolutions, Carroll County, 49
Deep Run School, 139
Deer Creek, 12, 64, 130, 131
Deer Park, 138
DeFord family, 87
Delaplaine Center for the Visual Arts, 64
Delaware Indians, 12
Democratic National Convention, 124
Democratic Party, 74
DeRan, David, 126
Detour, 53
Detrick, Dr. Frederick Louis, 107
Detrick Earth Station, 107
Devereaux, Mike, 105
Dickey, William J., 76
Diggs, Edward, 136

dinosaurs, 9, 96
District Court of Maryland, 66
Dixon, Jeremiah, 20
Dixon, James, 74
Dixon, Thomas, 74
Donovan, Artie, 84
Dorsey, John, 16
Dorsey, John, Jr., 98
Double Pipe Creek, 53
Douglas, Stephen A., 43
Dred Scott Decision, 103
Dubai World Cup race, 126
Dug Hill, 6
Dulany, Daniel, 15, 16, 94
Dulles Airport, 65, 66
Dundalk, 77
Dundalk Community College, 80

Early, General Jubal, 47, 52, 111
East Coast Telecommunications Center, 107
Eden, Father, 131
Eden Mill Nature Center, 131–2
Edgewood, 118, 127, 131
Edgewood Arsenal, 13, 58, 61, 62, 118, 122, 127, 128
education: Baltimore Co., 78–80; Carroll, 139–41; Frederick, 99–100; Harford, 120–1
Eighteenth Amendment, 55, 97
Eisenhower, David, 108
Eisenhower, President Dwight D., 108
Eldersburg, 134
Elkridge Hunt Club, 90
Elkridge Landing, 25
Elk Run Vineyard, 101, 144
Elk's Lodge, 52
Ellicott, Major Andrew, 82
Ellicott City, 91
Ellicott's Mills, 27, 82
Emerald Hill, 144
Emery Chapel School, 139
Emmit, Samuel, 96
Emmitsburg, 9, 69, 111
endangered animals, 7
endangered plants, 8, 105
endangered species, 135
England, 15, 18, 32, 34, 35, 37, 68
Erse O'Malley, 61
Essex, 66, 77, 88
Essex Community College, 80
Europe, 22, 73, 120
Eutaw Place Baptist Church (Baltimore City), 85